SMALL *Oxford* BOOKS

PARENTS &
CHILDREN

SMALL *Oxford* BOOKS

PARENTS & CHILDREN

Compiled by
CLAIRE TOMALIN

Oxford New York Toronto Melbourne
OXFORD UNIVERSITY PRESS
1981

Oxford University Press, Walton Street, Oxford OX2 6DP

London Glasgow New York Toronto
Delhi Bombay Calcutta Madras Karachi
Kuala Lumpur Singapore Hong Kong Tokyo
Nairobi Dar es Salaam Cape Town
Melbourne Wellington

and associate companies in
Beirut Berlin Ibadan Mexico City

British Library Cataloguing in Publication Data

Parents and children. — (Small Oxford books).
1. Parent and child — Literary collections
I. Tomalin, Claire
809'. 933520431   PN6071.P29/   80–42093

ISBN 0-19-214123-6

*

To the memory of
my daughter Susanna
1958 – 1980

Printed in Great Britain by
Hazell Watson & Viney Limited
Aylesbury, Bucks

Introduction

The voices of parents and children, describing, teaching, hoping, blaming, quarrelling, analysing or despairing of one another: this small anthology catches a few as it travels through nearly five hundred years of English life. Diaries, letters, sermons, poems, anecdotes, manuals, interviews and novels are freely mixed together, each with its own fragment or facet of truth, none conclusive, yet forming themselves into shapes and patterns.

In the earlier centuries the written record is scant; we are glimpsing brilliant highlights rather than a reflection of general experience. Did the poor and illiterate love their children less than we do, as some historians suggest? Probably not; but hardship and high infant mortality must have had their daunting effect on the attachment between parent and child. Even among the rich a system of wet nurses in infancy and the sending of children from home before adolescence – complained of by the Venetian ambassador on the first page here – must have blunted feelings on both sides. The prodigious death rate among parents as well as children may also have had its bearing on what either group dared to expect: and expectations are what people write about most often in human relations. Yet at all times there have plainly been fathers and mothers who took a spontaneous and passionate delight in their children, as Thomas More did in his, or Lady Barnard in the ballad of *Gil Morice*; at all times parents have suffered from the precariousness of their children's lives, as Ben Jonson did.

A few historical landmarks coincide with some shifts of tone. The middle of the sixteenth century saw the establishment of parish registers in which every child's birth was recorded, in theory at least. About the same time, in 1554, Thomas Phaire published the first paediatric textbook in English, *The Boke of Chyldren*; it went into seven editions. These were signs that God's gifts of life and death were under scrutiny by mankind, and even disputed. A little over a hundred years later, the execution of Charles I and then the publication of *Paradise Lost* could each be said to have played a part in subverting the patriarchal authority which had preached obedience and submission as the cardinal virtues in subjects, angels and children alike.

From this point there are two diverging strands. One, with Locke as theoretician, is predominantly humanist, its stress on the pleasures of family affection that supports and encourages the child. (In painting, its apotheosis comes with the secular mother and baby portraits and family groups of Romney and Reynolds.) The story of Lord Holland allowing his small son Charles James Fox to ride on the saddle of mutton with his feet in the gravy shows how far this tendency could go. 'Let nothing be done to break his spirit. The world will do that business fast enough,' was Lord Holland's view.

The other strand continued rather grimly the tradition of parent as God-surrogate. Hence Susanna Wesley's insistence on the importance of breaking the will of the child, an insistence echoed by the educationalist Hannah More a hundred years after Mrs Wesley. It is not surprising that the two great nineteenth century rebels against the family, Percy Bysshe Shelley and Samuel Butler, both saw their struggles in terms of fighting off orthodox Christianity as well as their fathers' authority.

And mothers? The most touching sound arising from these pages is probably the dawn chorus of newly literate mothers singing as the Enlightenment sun rises over the eighteenth century. Suddenly women can pick up their pens and begin to describe their children and what they feel for them. There is a gush of sensibility, but also some good sense: science is allowed to save the little ones from smallpox, and the spirit of scientific inquiry also encourages careful observation of childish behaviour. The wisdom and even the mistakes of children are now thought worthy of attention: *we* can learn from *them*. Fanny Burney's elderly father urges her to 'infantine biography' with the remark, 'Poor Boswell is gone! But his method of recording the colloquial wisdom of a *great man* is a good one – try it upon a little one!'

With this much value placed upon him, the child's vulnerability to neglect and cruelty takes on a new aspect. Writers become social reformers, chimney sweeps and Poor House boys find their champions. At the same time the child is promoted to a position of moral power in fiction: his eye at the centre of a novel spies out parental weakness and injustice, and the pleasures of vengeance, of turning the tables on once tyrannical figures, are manifest in much nineteenth- and twentieth-century fiction.

By the middle of the present century, parental failure has been so thoroughly investigated that al-most everyone is ready to plead guilty. Freud's account of the development of the infant was not reassuring, and Thomas Phaire's American successor Dr Spock (a best-seller in England) felt obliged to preface his remarks on child care by telling parents they might safely trust their own instincts. But even when they did they might be displeased with the result. Margaret

Drabble shows the mother as a confident, protective tigress, but in Beryl Bainbridge the destructive power of the child has become too much for the mother to confront.

In the 1970s the historian E. P. Thompson suggested that we are finding it increasingly difficult to imagine any future for our species; and Philip Larkin's view of propagation must be the grimmest ever set down by a poet. 'The fathers have eaten sour grapes, and the children's teeth are set on edge': perhaps it says something about contemporary attitudes that in my search for something less black to round off the anthology I came across several accounts by child-care specialists of what a good relationship between parent and child *ought* to be, but failed to find a poem or story that presented one. Instead, I found a joke; and, after all, the parent-child power-scale may be best balanced with a wry smile.

Probably the first foreign comment on English parents comes from a Venetian envoy to the court of Henry VII in 1497. Neither his name nor the recipient of his Relation of the Island of England is known, and for many years it remained in the Abbate Canonici library in Venice; but in 1804 it was privately printed by the Earl of Macartney, and in 1847 translated by Charlotte Sneyd and published by the Camden Society.

The want of affection in the English is strongly manifested towards their children; for after having kept them at home till they arrive at the age of 7 or 9 years at the utmost, they put them out, both males and females, to hard service in the houses of other people, binding them generally for another 7 or 9 years. And these are called apprentices, and during that time they perform all the most menial offices; and few are born who are exempted from this fate, for every one, however rich he may be, sends away his children into the houses of others, whilst he, in return, receives those of strangers into his own. And on inquiring their reason for this severity, they answered that they did it in order that their children might learn better manners. But I, for my part, believe that they do it because they like to enjoy all their comforts themselves, and that they are better served by strangers than they would be by their own children.

This next extract in which Sir Thomas More greets his beloved children, Margaret, Elizabeth, Cecilia and John, is taken from his Latin verses, probably written in 1517 when he went to Calais; his children were then still young, and their mother had died while they were babies.

I hope that a letter to all of you may find my four children in good health and that your father's good wishes may keep you so. In the meantime, while I make a long journey, drenched by a soaking rain, and while my mount, too frequently, is bogged down in the mud, I compose these verses for you in the hope that, although unpolished, they may give you pleasure. From them you may gather an indication of your father's feelings for you – how much more than his own eyes he loves you; for the mud, miserably stormy weather, and the necessity for driving a diminutive horse through deep waters have not been able to distract his thoughts from you or to prevent his proving that, wherever he is, he thinks of you. For instance, when – and it is often – his horse stumbles and threatens to fall, your father is not interrupted in the composition of his verses. Poetry often springs from a heart which has no feeling; these verses a father's love provides – along with a father's natural anxiety. It is not so strange that I love you with my whole heart, for being a father is not a tie which can be ignored. Nature in her wisdom has attached the parent to the child and bound them spiritually together with a Herculean knot. This tie is the source of my consideration for your immature minds, a consideration which causes me to take you often into my arms. This tie is the reason why I regularly fed you cake and gave you ripe apples and pears. This tie is the reason why I used to dress you in silken garments and why I never could endure to hear you cry. You know, for example, how often I kissed you, how seldom I whipped you. My whip was invariably a peacock's tail. Even this I wielded hesitantly and gently so that sorry welts might not disfigure your tender seats. Brutal and unworthy to be called father is he who does not weep himself at the tears of his child. How other fathers act I do not know, but you know well how gentle and devoted is my manner towards you, for I have always profoundly loved my own children and I have always been an indulgent parent – as every father ought to be. But at this moment my love has increased so much that it seems to me I used not to love you at all. This feeling of mine is produced by your adult manners, adult despite your tender years; by your instincts, trained in noble principles which must be learned; by your pleasant way of speaking, fashioned for clarity; and by your very careful weighing of every word. These characteristics of yours so strangely tug at my heart, so closely bind me to you, my children, that my being your father (the only reason for many a father's love) is hardly a reason at all for my love of you. Therefore, most dearly beloved children all, continue to endear yourselves to your father and, by those same accomplishments which make me think that I had not loved you before, make me think hereafter (for you can do it) that I do not love you now.

Leicester Bradner and C. Arthur Lynch (translators),
Latin Epigrams of Thomas More, 1953

Sir Thomas More was executed in 1535, and his son-in-law, William Roper, wrote his Life *soon afterwards, although it was not printed until 1626.*

When Sir Thomas More came from Westminster to the Tower-ward again, his daughter, my wife, desirous to see her father, whom she thought she should never see in this world after, and also to have his final blessing, gave attendance about the Tower Wharf, where she knew he should pass by, before he could enter into the Tower. There tarrying for his coming, as soon as she saw him, after his blessing upon her knees reverently received, she hasting towards him, and without consideration or care of herself, pressing in among the midst of the throng and company of the guard, that with halberds and bills went round about him, hastily ran to him, and there openly in the sight of them all, embraced him, took him about the neck and kissed him. Who well liking her most natural and dear daughterly affection towards him, gave her his fatherly blessing, and many godly words of comfort besides. From whom after she was departed, she not satisfied with her former sight of him, and like one that had forgotten herself, being all ravished with the entire love of her dear father, having respect neither to herself, nor to the press of the people and the multitude that were about him, suddenly turned back again, ran to him as before, took him about the neck, and divers times together most lovingly kissed him; and at last, with a full heavy heart, was fain to depart from him: the beholding whereof was to many of them that were present thereat so lamentable, that it made them for very sorrow thereof to mourn and weep.

More wrote his last letter to his daughter in the Tower, with a piece of coal, on 5 July 1535:

I never liked your manner toward me better than when

you kissed me last; for I love when daughterly love and dear charity hath no leisure to look for worldly courtesy. Farewell, my dear child, and pray for me, and I shall for you and all your friends, that we may merrily meet in heaven...

§

Lady Jane Grey was so well schooled that she thanked God for her 'sharp and severe' parents.

When I am in the presence of either father or mother, whether I speak, keep silence, sit, stand or go, eat, drink, be merry or sad, be sewing, playing, dancing, or doing anything else, I must do it, as it were, in such weight, measure and number, even so perfectly as God made the world, or else I am so sharply taunted, so cruelly threatened, yea presently sometimes with pinches, nips and bobs, and other ways which I will not name for the honour I bear them, so without measure misordered that I think myself in hell till time come that I must go to Mister Elmer who teacheth me so gently and pleasantly, with such fair allurement to learning that I think all the time nothing while I am with him. And when I am called from him, I fall on weeping.

From Roger Ascham, *The Scholemaster*, 1570

This poem is thought to be addressed to Ralegh's elder son Walter, born in 1593: Ralegh's editor, Agnes Latham, suggests it might be 'an Elizabethan nursery joke'.

SIR WALTER RALEGH TO HIS SON

Three things there be that prosper up apace
And flourish, whilst they grow asunder far,
But on a day, they meet all in one place,
And when they meet, they one another mar;

And they be these, the wood, the weed, the wag.
The wood is that, which makes the Gallow tree,
The weed is that, which strings the Hangman's bag,
The wag my pretty knave betokeneth thee.
Mark well dear boy whilst these assemble not,
Green springs the tree, hemp grows, the wag is wild,
But when they meet, it makes the timber rot,
It frets the halter, and it chokes the child.
   Then bless thee, and beware, and let us pray
   We part not with thee at this meeting day.

John Aubrey's story of the Raleghs, father and son, casts a somewhat different light on them. Aubrey claimed that his Lives, *written in the late seventeenth century when he himself was in his fifties, were 'the naked and plain trueth' adding that an editor might want to 'sowe-on some Figge-leaves'.*

My old friend James Harrington, Esq., was well acquainted with Sir Benjamin Ruddyer, who was an acquaintance of Sir Walter Ralegh's. He told Mr J. H. that Sir Walter Ralegh, being invited to dinner with some great person, where his son was to goe with him: He sayd to his Son, Thou art such a quarrelsome, affronting creature that I am ashamed to have such a Beare in my Company. Mr Walt. humbled himselfe to his Father, and promised he would behave himselfe mightily mannerly. So away they went, and Sir Benjamin, I thinke, with them. He sate next to his Father and was very demure at leaste halfe dinner time. Then sayd he, I this morning, not having the feare of God before my eies, but by the instigation of the devill, went to a Whore. I was very eager of her, kissed and embraced her, and went to enjoy her, but she thrust me from her, and vowed I should not, *For your father lay with me but an hower ago.* Sir Walt, being so strangely supprized and putt out of his countenance at so great a Table, gives his son a damned blow over the face; his son, as rude as he was, would not strike his father, but strikes over the face of the Gentleman that sate next to him, and sayed, *Box about, 'twill come to my Father anon.* 'Tis now a common used Proverb.

John Aubrey, *Brief Lives*, 1669–96

ON MY FIRST SON

Farewell, thou child of my right hand, and joy;
  My sin was too much hope of thee, lov'd boy,
Seven years tho'wert lent to me, and I thee pay,
  Exacted by thy fate, on the just day.
O, could I lose all father now. For why
  Will man lament the state he should envie?
To have so soon scap'd worlds, and flesh's rage,
  And, if no other misery, yet age?
Rest in soft peace, and, ask'd, say here doth lie
  Ben. Jonson his best piece of *poetry*.
For whose sake, henceforth, all his vows be such,
  As what he loves may never like too much.

Ben Jonson, 1572–1637

Francis Quarles's description of the infant Jesus must owe something to his own experience: he was the father of eighteen children.

from ON THE INFANCY OF OUR SAVIOUR

O! what a ravishment't had been, to see
Thy little *Saviour* perking on thy *Knee*!
To see him nuzzle in thy *Virgin* Breast;
His milk-white body all unclad, undressed!
To see thy busy Fingers clothe and wrap
His spradling Limbs in thy indulgent *Lap*!

To see his desperate *Eyes*, with Childish grace,
Smiling upon his smiling Mother's face!
And, when his forward strength began to bloom,
To see him *diddle* up and down the Room!

Divine Fancies, Book I, 1632

This passage from the diary of Ralph Josselin, an East Anglian clergyman, schoolmaster and father of ten, describes the birth of his seventh child to his wife Jane, in 1658.

Jan 12 1658 Baptized my neighbour Burtons son, at night the midwife with us, my wife thinking shee might use her, but being sent for my wife let her goe, that another that was in present need might bee holpen, and it was a mercy to us so to dispose my wives heart, her going tending to save a poore womans life, but within halfe an houre, as soon as I had done family prayer, my wife had so sure a signe of her labour and speedie that put us all to a plunge, I sent 2 messengers after her and it was at least 4 houres before shee came . . . . My wife was wonderfully afraid and amazed but helpe was speedily with her and in particular young Mrs Harlakenden [the squire's wife], who put forth her selfe to the utmost to helpe her, and her presence was much to my wife.

Jan 13 her pains ceased, the labour very strange to her, which sett her heart, but her eye was towards him who is the helper, my faith was up for her, shee judged at the labour it would be a daughter, contrary to all her former experience and thought; prayer was for her; wee comended her to god and her warm bed early and all to their rests, none watching this night as formerly. Her sleep was a comfort to her mixed with pain, feare, which made her quake and tremble.

14 and so increased on by two of the clocke in this morning that I called up the midwife, and nurse, gott

[8]

fires and all redie, and then her labour came on so strongly and speedily that the child was borne only 2 or 3 women more gott in to her but god supplied all, young Mrs Harlakenden gott up to us very speedily, and some others; my wives labour was different from all former exceeding sharpe, shee judged her midwife did not doe her part, but god did all, and hath given us new experience of his goodness, the child was dead when borne, I blesse god who recovered it to life, wee baptized it this day by the name of Mary, young Mrs Harlakenden holding it up in my wives place god hath evened my number and made up the three which he tooke from mee my heart was very lightsom and joyful in the god of my mercies.

ed. Alan McFarlane

And these are the words of Lady Frances Hatton to her husband in 1678 at the birth of her third daughter:

I am sure you will love it though it be a Girle and I trust in God I may live to bring you boys.

She did not live to give him boys but he got them from a later wife.

UPON THE DISOBEDIENT CHILD

Children, when little, how do they delight us!
When they grow bigger, they begin to fright us.
Their sinful nature prompts them to rebel,
And to delight in paths that lead to hell.
Their parents' love and care they overlook,
As if relation had them quite forsook.
They take the counsels of the wanton, rather
Than the most grave instructions of a father,
They reckon parents ought to do for them,
Though they the fifth commandment do contemn.
They snap, and snarl, if parents them controul,
Although in things most hurtful to the soul,
They reckon they are masters, and that we
Who parents are, should to them subject be.

John Bunyan, *Divine Emblems*, 1686

From an anonymous carol, already known in the seventeenth century.

Joseph was an old man,
    And an old man was he,
When he wedded Mary
    In the land of Galilee.

Joseph and Mary walked
    Through an orchard good,
Where was cherries and berries
    So red as any blood.

Joseph and Mary walked
    Through an orchard green,
Where was berries and cherries
    As thick as might be seen.

O then bespoke Mary,
    So meek and so mild,
'Pluck me one cherry, Joseph,
    For I am with child.'

O then bespoke Joseph
   With words so unkind,
'Let him pluck thee a cherry
   That brought thee with child.'

O then bespoke the babe
   Within his mother's womb,
'Bow down then the tallest tree
   For my mother to have some.'

Then bowed down the highest tree
   Unto his mother's hand:
Then she cried, 'See, Joseph,
   I have cherries at command!'

§

*Gil Morice is the subject of an old Scottish ballad. He is
the natural son of Lady Barnard; a message he has sent
his mother leads Lord Barnard to suppose him his wife's
lover; Lord Barnard goes out jealously to kill him.*

Nae wonder, nae wonder, Gil Morice,
   My lady loed thee weel,
The fairest part of my bodie
   Is blacker than thy heel.
Yet neir the less now, Gil Morice,
   For a' thy great beautie,
Ye's rew the day ye eir was born;
   That head sall gae wi' me.

Now he has drawn his trusty brand,
   And slaited on the strae;†
And thro' Gil Morice' fair body
   He's gar caould iron gae.
And he has tain Gil Morice' head
   And set it on a speir;
The meanest man in a' his train
   Has gotten that head to bear.

† slaited on the strae] sharpened on the grass

And he has tain Gil Morice up,
    Laid him across his steid,
And brocht him to his painted bowr
    And laid him on a bed.
The lady sat on castil wa',
    Beheld baith dale and doun;
And there she saw Gil Morice' head
    Cum trailing to the toun.

Far better I loe that bluidy head,
    Both and that yellow hair,
Than Lord Barnard, and a' his lands,
    As they lig here and thair.
And she has tain her Gil Morice,
    And kissd baith mouth and chin:
I was once as fow of Gil Morice,
    As the hip is o' the stean.

I got ye in my father's house,
    Wi' mickle sin and shame;
I brocht thee up in gude grene wode,
    Under the heavy rain.
Oft have I by thy cradle sitten,
    And fondly seen thee sleip;
But now I gae about they grave,
    The saut tears for to weip.

And syne† she kissd his bluidy cheik,
    And syne his bluidy chin:
O better I loe my Gil Morice
    Than a' my kith and kin!
Away, away, ye ill woman,
    And an il deith mait ye dee:
Gin I had kend he'd bin your son,
    He'd neir bin slain for mee.

Percy's Reliques, Third Series, Book I, 1765

† syne] then

[12]

JOHN LOCKE

John Locke's Some Thoughts Concerning Education *began as a series of letters written at the request of his friend Edward Clarke, who wanted advice on the upbringing of his son in the 1680s. It was first published in 1693 and reprinted steadily throughout the eighteenth century. Locke laid particular stress on the independence of mind of the child, on his need for 'childish actions and gaiety of carriage, which, whilst he is very young is as necessary to him as meat or sleep', and on the importance of tenderness in every aspect of education. He did not believe in breaking spirits, and he wished parents to consult reason rather than custom.*

Begin therefore betimes nicely to observe your son's temper; and that, when he is under least restraint, in his play, and as he thinks out of your sight. See what are his predominant passions, and prevailing inclinations; whether he be fierce or mild, bold or bashful, compassionate or cruel, open or reserved, etc. For as these are different in him, so are your methods to be different, and your authority must hence take measures to apply itself different ways to him. These native propensities, these prevalences of constitution, are not to be cured by rules, or a direct contest; especially those of them that are the humbler and meaner sort, which proceed from fear, and lowness of spirit; though with art they may be much mended, and turned to good purposes. But this, be sure, after all is done, the bias will always hang on that side, that nature first placed it: and if you carefully observe the characters of his mind, now in the first scenes of his life, you will ever after be able to judge which way his thoughts lean, and what he aims at, even hereafter, when, as he grows up, the plot thickens, and he puts on several shapes to act it.

I must here take the liberty to mind parents of this

one thing, viz. that he that will have his son have a respect for him, and his orders, must himself have a great reverence for his son.

Susanna Wesley, the twenty-fifth and last child of Dr Annesley, a Nonconformist London Divine, was born in 1669. At the age of thirteen she demonstrated her considerable will-power by joining the Church of England, which had persecuted her father. She married Samuel Wesley, a parson, in 1689 and moved to Lincolnshire where she bore nineteen children and brought up ten, enduring ill-health and poverty (Samuel was imprisoned for debt on one occasion). Her home was of necessity run on the lines of a small boarding-school. She lived to see her sons John and Charles responsible for the Methodist revival; interestingly, John claimed that he had never in his childhood understood 'inward obedience or holiness'. She died in 1742, with John at her side, and, although she was still an Anglican, was buried among the Puritan Saints in Bunhill Fields.

In the summer of 1732 John wrote to his mother asking her to explain her method of child-rearing; this passage is taken from her reply.

Epworth, July 24th, 1732.

Dear Son, – According to your desire, I have collected the principal rules I observed in educating my family.

The children were always put into a regular method of living, in such things as they were capable of, from their birth; as in dressing and undressing, changing their linen, etc. The first quarter commonly passed in sleep. After that, they were, if possible, laid into their cradle awake, and rocked to sleep, and so they were kept rocking until it was time for them to awake. This was done to bring them to a regular course of sleeping, which at first was three hours in the morning, and three in the afternoon; afterwards two hours, till they needed none at all. When turned a year old (and some before) they were taught to fear the rod and to cry softly, by which means they escaped abundance of correction which they might otherwise have had, and that most odious noise of crying of children was rarely heard in the house, but the family usually lived in as much quietness as if there had not been a child among them.

As soon as they had grown pretty strong they were confined to three meals a day. At dinner their little table and chairs were set by ours, where they could be overlooked; and they were suffered to eat and drink (small beer) as much as they would, but not to call for anything. If they wanted aught they used to whisper to the maid that attended them, who came and spake to me; and as soon as they could handle a knife and fork they were set to our table. They were never suffered to choose their meat, but always made to eat such things as were provided for the family. Mornings they always had spoon-meat; sometimes at nights. But whatever they had, they were never permitted at those meals to eat of more than one thing, and of that sparingly enough. Drinking or eating between meals was never allowed, unless in case of sickness, which seldom happened. Nor were they suffered to go into the kitchen to ask anything of the servants when they were at meat: if it was known they did so, they were certainly beat, and the servants severely reprimanded.

At six, as soon as family prayer was over, they had their supper; at seven the maid washed them, and, beginning at the youngest, she undressed and got them all to bed by eight, at which time she left them in their several rooms awake, for there was no such thing allowed of in our house as sitting by a child till it fell asleep.

They were so constantly used to eat and drink what

was given them that when any of them was ill there was no difficulty in making them take the most unpleasant medicine; for they durst not refuse it, though some of them would presently throw it up. This I mention to show that a person may be taught to take anything, though it be never so much against his stomach.

In order to form the minds of children, the first thing to be done is to conquer their will and bring them to an obedient temper. To inform the understanding is a work of time, and must with children proceed by slow degrees, as they are able to bear it; but the subjecting of the will is a thing which must be done at once. . . . When a child is corrected it must be conquered; and this will be no hard matter to do, if it be not grown headstrong by too much indulgence. And when the will of a child is totally subdued, and it is brought to revere and stand in awe of the parents, then a great many childish follies and inadvertencies may be passed by. . . . I insist upon the conquering the will of children betimes, because this is the only strong and rational foundation of a religious education. . . .

Lord Chesterfield wrote almost daily to his illegitimate son Philip Stanhope. Of these two letters, the first was written when the boy was ten, the second nearly a year later.

Bath, October 4, 1738

My Dear Child: By my writing so often, and by the manner in which I write, you will easily see that I do not treat you as a little child, but as a boy who loves to learn, and is ambitious of receiving instructions. I am even persuaded, that, in reading my letters, you are attentive, not only to the subject of which they treat, but likewise to the orthography and to the style. It is of the greatest importance to write letters well; as this is a talent which unavoidably occurs every day of one's life, as well in business as in pleasure; and inaccuracies in orthography or in style are never pardoned but in ladies. When you are older, you will read the 'Epistles' (that is to say Letters) of Cicero; which are the most perfect models of good writing. *A propos* Cicero, I must give you some account of him. [He goes on to explain who Cicero was and what an orator is, and a little Roman history, finishing his letter:]

In case there should be any words in my letters which you do not perfectly understand, remember always to inquire the explanation from your mamma, or else to seek for them in the dictionary. Adieu.

Isleworth, September 19, 1739

My Dear Child: I am very well pleased with your last letter. The writing was very good, and the promise you make exceedingly fine. You must keep it, for an honest man never breaks his word. You engage to retain the instructions which I give you. That is sufficient, for though you do not properly comprehend them at present, age and reflection will, in time, make you understand them.

With respect to the contents of your letter, I believe you have had proper assistance; indeed, I do not as yet expect that you can write a letter without help. You ought, however, to try, for nothing is more requisite than to write a good letter. Nothing in fact is more easy. Most persons who write ill, do so because they aim at writing better than they can, by which means they acquire a formal and unnatural style. Whereas, to write well, we must write easily and naturally. For instance, if you want to write a letter to me, you should only consider what you would say if you were with me, and then write it in plain terms, just as if you were conversing. I will suppose, then, that you sit down to write to me unassisted, and I imagine your letter would probably be much in these words: –

My Dear Papa: I have been at Mr Maittaire's this morning, where I have translated English into Latin and Latin into English, and so well, that at the end of my excerise he has writ *optime*. I have likewise repeated a Greek verb, and pretty well. After this I ran home, like a little WILD BOY, and played till dinnertime. This became a serious task, for I ate like a wolf: and by that you may judge that I am in very good health. Adieu.

Well, sir, the above is a good letter, and yet very easily written, because it is exceedingly natural. Endeavour then sometimes to write to me of yourself, without minding either the beauty of the writing or the straightness of the lines. Take as little trouble as possible. By that means you will by degrees use yourself to write perfectly well, and with ease. Adieu. Come to me tomorrow at twelve, or Friday morning at eight o'clock.

THOMAS HOLCROFT

Thomas Holcroft was born in 1745, when his family inhabited a basement room in Leicester Square. The anecdotes here relate to the 1750s, when they had moved to the country.

My father was very fond, and not a little vain, of me. He delighted to shew how much I was superior to other children, and this propensity had sometimes a good effect. One evening when it was quite dark, daylight having entirely disappeared, and the night being cloudy, he was boasting to a neighbour of my courage; and his companion seeming rather to doubt, my father replied, he would put it immediately to the proof. 'Tom,' said he, 'you must go to the house of Farmer such a one,' (I well remember the walk, but not the name of the person,) 'and ask whether he goes to London to morrow.' I was startled, but durst not dispute his authority, it was too great over me, besides that my vanity to prove my valor was not a little excited: accordingly I took my hat, and immediately obeyed.

The house I was sent to, as far as I can remember, must have been between a quarter and half a mile distant; and the road that led to it, was by the side of the hedge on the left hand of the Common. However, I knew the way well enough, and proceeded; but it was with many stops, starts, and fears. It may be proper to observe here, that although I could not have been without courage, yet I was really, when a child, exceedingly apprehensive, and full of superstition. When I saw magpies, it denoted good or ill luck, according as they did or did not cross me. When walking, I pored for pins, or rusty nails; which, if they lay in certain directions, foreboded some misfortune. Many such whims possessed my brain – I was therefore not at all free from notions of this kind, on the present occasion.

However, I went forward on my errand, humming, whistling, and looking as carefully as I could; now and then making a false step, which helped to relieve me, for it obliged me to attend to the road. When I came to the farm-house, I delivered my message. 'Bless me, child,' cried the people within, 'have you come, this dark night, all alone?' 'Oh yes,' I said, assuming an air of self-consequence. 'And who sent you?' 'My father wanted to *know*,' I replied equivocally. One of them then offered to take me home, but of this I would by no means admit. My whole little stock of vanity was roused, and I hastily scampered out of the house, and was hidden in the dark. My return was something, but not much less alarming than my journey thither. At last I got safely home, glad to be rid of my fears, and inwardly not a little elated with my success. 'Did you hear or see any body, Tom,' said my father, 'as you went or came back?' 'No,' said I, 'it was quite dark; not but I thought once or twice, I did hear something behind me.' In fact, it was my father and his companion, who had followed me at a little distance. This, my father, in fondly praising me for my courage, some time after told me.

I cannot say what my father's employment was, while I and my mother were, what they emphatically called *tramping* the villages, to hawk our pedlary. It may be presumed, however, that it was not very lucrative, for he soon after left it, and he and my mother went into the country, hawking their small wares, and dragging me after them. They went first to Cambridge, and afterwards, as their hopes of success led them, traversed the neighbouring villages. Among these we came to one which I thought most remarkably clean, well built, and unlike villages in general: my father said it was the handsomest in the kingdom. We must have been very

poor, however, and hard-driven on this occasion; for
here it was that I was either encouraged, or commanded,
one day to go by myself, from house to house, and beg.
Young as I was, I had considerable readiness in making
out a story, and on this day, my little inventive faculties
shone forth with much brilliancy. I told one story at
one house, another at another, and continued to vary
my tale just as the suggestions arose: the consequence
of which was, that I moved the good country people
exceedingly. One called me a poor fatherless child:
another exclaimed, what a pity! I had so much sense! a
third patted my head, and prayed God to preserve me,
that I might make a good man. And most of them
contributed either by scraps of meat, farthings, bread
and cheese, or other homely offers, to enrich me, and
send me away with my pockets loaded. I joyfully
brought as much of my stores as I could carry, to the
place of rendezvous my parents had appointed, where I
astonished them by again reciting the false tales I had
so readily invented. My father, whose passions were
easily moved, felt no little conflict of mind as I proceeded. I can now, in imagination, see the working of
his features. 'God bless the boy! I never heard the
like!' Then turning to my mother, he exclaimed with
great earnestness – 'This must not be! the poor child
will become a common place liar! A hedge-side
rogue! – He will learn to pilfer! – Turn a confirmed
vagrant! – Go on the high way when he is older, and
get hanged. He shall never go on such errands again.'
How fortunate for me in this respect, that I had such a
father! He was driven by extreme poverty, restless
anxiety, and a brain too prone to sanguine expectation,
into many absurdities, which were but the harbingers of
fresh misfortunes: but he had as much integrity and
honesty of heart as perhaps any man in the kingdom,
who had had no greater advantages. It pleases me

now to recollect, that, though I had a consciousness that my talents could keep my parents from want, I had a still stronger sense of the justice of my father's remarks.

Later Holcroft became a Newmarket stable boy, an actor, translator, novelist, passionate radical and believer in the perfectibility of human nature through education. Tragically, his own son became delinquent and killed himself.

Holcroft died in 1809 and Hazlitt published his unfinished memoirs, from which these passages are taken, a year later.

§

William Blake's little chimney sweeper appears in the Songs of Experience *of 1794, and his accusation of his parents is confirmed by the words of a master chimney sweep, David Porter, in 1798: 'Half of the climbing boys are now purchased from needy and illiterate parents'.*

THE CHIMNEY SWEEPER

A little black thing among the snow:
Crying weep, weep, in notes of woe!
Where are thy father & mother? say?
They are both gone up to the church to pray.

Because I was happy upon the heath,
And smil'd among the winters snow:
They clothed me in the clothes of death,
And taught me to sing the notes of woe.

And because I am happy, & dance & sing,
They think they have done me no injury:
And are gone to praise God & his Priest & King
Who make up a heaven of our misery.

This anecdote from the Life of George Crabbe *(1834) by the poet's son describes the father's vulnerable childhood and is set in the 1760s.*

Walking one day in the street, he chanced to displease a stout lad, who doubled his fist to beat him; but another boy interfered to claim benefit of clergy for the studious George. 'You must not meddle with *him*,' he said; 'let *him* alone, for he ha' got l'arning.'

His father observed this bookish turn, and though he had then no higher view of him in life than that he should follow his own example, and be employed in some inferior department of the revenue service, he resolved to give George the advantage of passing some time in a school at Bungay, on the borders of Norfolk, where it was hoped the activity of his mind would be disciplined into orderly diligence. I cannot say how soon this removal from the paternal roof took place; but it must have been very early, as the following anecdote will show: – The first night he spent at Bungay he retired to bed, he said, 'with a heavy heart, thinking of his fond, indulgent mother'. But the morning brought a new misery. The slender and delicate child had hitherto been dressed by his mother. Seeing the other boys begin to dress themselves, poor George, in great confusion, whispered to his bedfellow, 'Master G——, can you put on your shirt? – for – for I'm afraid I cannot.'

The younger Crabbe's journey to Suffolk must be one of the earliest accounts of a family jaunt in which the enjoyment of the child was a paramount consideration.

Never can I forget my first excursion into Suffolk, in company with my parents. It was in the month of September, 1790 – (shortly after my mother had recovered from her confinement with her fourth son,

Edmund Crabbe, who died in his sixth year) – that, dressed in my first suit of boy's clothes (and that scarlet), in the height of a delicious season, I was mounted beside them in their huge old gig, and visited the scenes and the persons familiar to me, from my earliest nursery days, in their conversation and anecdotes. Sometimes, as we proceeded, my father read aloud; sometimes he left us for a while to botanise among the hedgerows, and returned with some unsightly weed or bunch of moss, to him precious. Then, in the evening, when we had reached our inn, the happy child, instead of being sent early as usual to bed, was permitted to stretch himself on the carpet, while the reading was resumed, blending with sounds which, from novelty, appeared delightful – the buzzing of the bar, the rattling of wheels, the horn of the mail-coach, the gay glamour of the streets – everything to excite and astonish, in the midst of safety and repose. My father's countenance at such moments is still before me; with what gentle sympathy did he seem to enjoy the happiness of childhood!

*James Boswell (1740–95), Laird of Auchinleck, Edin-
burgh lawyer, perpetual seeker after father-figures (and
women), great biographer of Samuel Johnson, was also
one of the great diarists, as these entries concerning his
feelings for his father and children show.*

Monday 9th October 1775

My wife having been seized with her pains in the night,
I got up about three o'clock, and between four and
five Dr Young came. He and I sat upstairs mostly till
between three and four, when, after we had dined, her
labour became violent. I was full of expectation, and
meditated curiously on the thought that it was already
certain of what sex the child was, but that I could not
have the least guess on which side the probability was.
Miss Preston attended my wife close. Lady Preston
came several times to inquire, but did not go into the
room. I did not feel so much anxiety about my wife
now as on former occasions, being better used to an
inlying. Yet the danger was as great now as ever. I was
easier from the same deception which affects a soldier
who has escaped in several battles. She was very ill.
Between seven and eight I went into the room. She was
just delivered. I heard her say, 'God be thanked for
whatever he sends.' I supposed then the child was a
daughter. But she herself had not then seen it. Miss
Preston said, 'Is it a daughter?' 'No,' said Mrs Forrest,
the nurse-keeper, 'it's a son.' When I had seen the
little man I said that I should now be so anxious that
probably I should never again have an easy hour. I
said to Dr Young with great seriousness, 'Doctor,
Doctor, let no man set his heart upon anything in this
world but land or heritable bonds; for he has no
security that anything else will last as long as himself.'
My anxiety subdued a flutter of joy which was in my
breast. I wrote several letters to announce my son's

birth. I indulged some imaginations that he might perhaps be a great man.

Thursday 4th January 1776

... In the afternoon I was quite charmed with Veronica [his daughter]. She could now sing a number of tunes: Carrickfergus, O'er the Water to Charlie, Johnnie McGill, Wee Willy Gray, Nancy Dawson, Paddy Wake, Ploughman Laddie, Brose and Butter, O'er the Hills and Far Away. It was really extraordinary that a child not three years old should have such a musical memory, and she sung with a sweet voice and fine ear (if that expression be just). She could speak a great many words, but in an imperfect manner: 'Etti me see u picture' (Let me see your picture.) She could not pronounce 'f'. 'I heed.' (I'm feared. English, I'm afraid.) She rubbed my sprained ankle this afternoon with rum, with care and tenderness. With eager affection I cried, 'God bless you, my dearest little creature.' She answered, 'Od bess u, Papa.' Yet she loved her mother more than me, I suppose because her behaviour to her was more uniform.

Tuesday 6th February 1776

I had dreamt in the night that my father was dead. All the natural affection and tenderness of my younger years was revived in sleep. I was much distressed and I awaked crying. My mind was much softened. I was anxious to make my father easy and to have nothing in my conduct towards him of later years to regret after he was gone. My instantaneous thought was to go to him and agree to his entail directly. ... When I actually saw my father in the Court, his indifference froze my fine feelings.

The Vicar of Wakefield *by Oliver Goldsmith, published in 1776, is the* locus classicus *of the lost daughter. Here the Vicar is speaking to his wife Deborah.*

'I think myself happier now than the greatest monarch upon earth. He has no such fire-side, nor such pleasant faces about it. Yes, Deborah, we are now growing old; but the evening of our life is likely to be happy. We are descended from ancestors that knew no stain, and we shall leave a good and virtuous race of children behind us. While we live, they will be our support and our pleasure here; and when we die, they will transmit our honour untainted to posterity. Come, my son, we wait for a song: let us have a chorus. But where is my darling Olivia? That little cherub's voice is always sweetest in the concert.' Just as I spoke Dick came running in. 'O Papa, Papa, she is gone from us, she is gone from us for ever.' – 'Gone, child!' – 'Yes, she is gone off with two gentlemen in a post-chaise, and one of them kissed her, and said he would die for her: and she cried very much, and was for coming back; but he persuaded her again, and she went into the chaise, and said, 'O what will my poor Papa do when he knows I am undone!' – 'Now then,' cried I, 'my children go and be miserable: for we shall never enjoy one hour more. And O may Heaven's everlasting fury light upon him and his! – Thus to rob me of my child! – And sure it will, for taking back my sweet innocent that I was leading up to heaven. Such sincerity as my child was possessed of! – But all our earthly happiness is now over! Go my children, go and be miserable and in-famous; for my heart is broken within me!'

... The next morning we missed our wretched child at breakfast, where she used to give life and cheerfulness to us all. My wife ... attempted to ease her heart by reproaches. 'Never,' cried she, 'shall that vilest stain of our family again darken these harmless doors. I will never call her daughter more. No, let the strumpet live with her vile seducer: she may bring us to shame, but she shall never more deceive us.'

'Wife,' said I, 'do not talk thus hardly: my detestation of her guilt is as great as yours; but ever shall this house and this heart be open to a poor returning repentant sinner. The sooner she returns from her transgressions, the more welcome shall she be to me. For the first time the very best may err; art may persuade, and novelty spread out its charm. The first fault is the child of simplicity, but every other the offspring of guilt. Yes, the wretched creature shall be welcome to this heart and this house, though stained with ten thousand vices. I will again hearken to the music of her voice, again will I hang fondly on her bosom, if I find but repentance there. My son, bring hither my Bible and my staff: I will pursue her, wherever she is; and though I cannot save her from shame, I may prevent the continuance of iniquity.'

Hester Thrale, like Boswell, is chiefly famous for her friendship with Dr Johnson, who was devoted to her and took a keen interest in her children, of whom she had twelve. Six of them died before they were five, including the beloved and gifted Lucy; another tragedy was the death of Harry, the son and heir, at the age of nine. The other boy, Ralph, had a malformed brain and his death was a relief to his mother.

Mrs Thrale was passionately attached to her own mother, as is evident here. For her husband Thrale ('my master') she appears to have felt little. When she was widowed in her forties she married a man she loved at last, the Italian Piozzi; and with this act she forfeited the love and approval of both Dr Johnson and her daughters. At the age of forty-six she miscarried of a thirteenth child,

the first to be conceived in love, and grieved much for it.
Her Family Book, which Johnson encouraged her to keep,
is a minute record of her education of her children.

21 March 1773.

My Mother's Illness has lately increased so fast that it
has required all my Attention & shall have it – My
Children I shall keep, My Mother is leaving me, and
Filial Duty shall not be cheated of its due, what
Gratitude do I not owe her? what Esteem have I not of
Her? what Tenderness do I not feel for her? Oh my
sweet Mother! I have now past many days & Nights
in her room in her Room [*sic*], while Mr Thrale proceeded with his Affairs in London – they thank God do
mend every day, but nobody can guess what a Winter
this has been to me, & big with Child too again God
help me! This Morning therefore finding myself in-
capable of attending to every body, & every thing, I
fairly resolved to walk up the Common with Harry to
Dr Thomas who keeps a Boy's School here; & may at
least keep up that Knowledge he has, & perhaps get
more: he will likewise go on with his Writing more
commodiously there, while I give to my Mother my
undivided Attention; & She seems vastly delighted too
that She has lived to see him a School-boy. As for
Hetty, She already knows so much of History, Geo-
graphy, Astronomy & Natural Philosophy; that She
begins now to study for her own sake, & does not so
much require keeping to Hours as younger Children do;
She has besides a sort of every-day-Wit; a degree of
Prudence, Discretion and common Sense, that I have
seldom seen in a Girl even of twelve or thirteen Years
old, which makes her a most comfortable Child; in
spite of her bad Temper & cold heart; I really can
consult her and often do – She is so *very* rational.
[*Hetty was nine years old, Harry six at this time*]

23 July 1776.

Sophia Thrale is five Years old today; She Has read three Epistles & three Gospels: I do not make her get much by heart: The Thing is – I have really listened to Babies Learning till I am half stupefied – & all my pains have answered so poorly – I have no heart to battle with Sophy: She would probably learn very well, if I had the Spirit of teaching I once had, as She is docile & stout; able to bear buffeting & Confinement, & has withal reasonable good parts & a great Desire to please. But I will not make her Life miserable as I suppose it will be short – not for want of Health indeed, for no Girl can have better, but Harry and Lucy are dead, & why should Sophy live? The instructions I labor'd to give *them* – what did they end in? The Grave – & every recollection brings only new Regret. Sophy shall read well, & learn her Prayers; & take her Chance for more, when I can get it for her. At Present I can not begin battling with Babies – I have already spent my whole Youth at it & lost my Reward at last.

The written word came as easily to Fanny Burney as to Hester Thrale. She married at the age of forty-one in 1793, when she was already an established novelist; her husband d'Arblay was a French émigré, and their only son Alexander was born in December 1794. The following accounts of his weaning and inoculation come from her letters.

7 March 1795, to Mrs Waddington
Ah my Marianne! – What an age since I have written! – what delight – & what torture has filled up the interval – my Baby is all I can wish – my opening recovery was the most rapid I ever witnessed or heard of – but in a fortnight the poor thing had the Thrush – communicated it to my Breast – & in short – after torment

[30]

upon torment, a Milk fever ensued – an abscess in the Breast followed – & till that broke, 4 days ago, I suffered so as to make life – even My happy life – scarce my wish to preserve! – need I say more –

I am now fast recovering once more – living on Bark – Porter & raw Eggs – incessantly poured down – much reduced, you may believe – but free from pain & fever – Therefore in a fair way –

But – they have made me wean my Child! – O my Marianne! you who are so tender a Mother can need no words to say what that has cost me! But God be praised my Babe is well, feeds, while he pines – adieu – & Heaven bless you!

To her sister Susanna Phillips, 14 March 1797.
I would not awaken useless inquietude in your kind bosom by telling you our fixed design of innoculating our little love this spring – but Mr Ansell was bespoke a Week before this Letter was begun, & the last Day of last month he came – & performed the dreaded operation. The dear little soul sat on my lap, & he gave

him some Barley sugar; this made him consent to have his Frock taken off. Mr Ansell pressed me to relinquish him to Betty; but I could not to any one but his Father, who was at his field. When the Lancet was produced, Betty held him a favourite Toy, of which I began discoursing with him. It was a maimed young Drummer, of whose loss of Eyes, Nose, Chin & Hair he always hears with the tenderest interest. But, while listening attentively, he felt Mr Ansell grasp his arm to hold it steady – he turned quite away from his Drummer, & seeing the Lancet, shrunk back. Mr Ansell bid me help to hold him tight, – he then shriekt, & forcibly disengaged his arm from my hand – but, to my utter astonishment, held it out himself very quietly, & looked on, & suffered the incision to be made without a cry, or any resistance, only raising his Eyes from his Arm to Mr Ansell, with an expression of the most superlative wonder at his proceedings. Mr A. forced out the blood repeatedly, & played upon it with the Lancet for some minutes, fearing, he said, if particular caution was not used, the little soul was so pure his blood could not be infected. The Child still made no resistance, but looked at the blood with great curiosity in the most profound silent rumination. Mr Ansell still was apprehensive the disorder might not be imbibed, from the excessive strictness of his whole life's diet: he therefore asked my leave to innoculate the other arm also. I left it to his own decision, – & he took off the shirt from the other arm. – The little Creature fixed him very attentively, & then turned to me, as if for some explanation of such conduct; but still made not the smallest resistance, & without being held *at all*, permitted the second wound. – I own I could hardly endure the absence of his Father, to whom the actual view of this infantine courage and firmness would have been such exquisite delight. Mr Ansell confessed he had met no similar

instance. – You will not, I believe, expect an equal
history of his Mother's intrepidity – & therefore I pass
that bye. But she behaved *very well indeed* before
COMPANY!

... This stroke was given on the Tuesday; & on the
following Sunday, after Breakfasting with us in a
gaiety the most animating, & with Eyes & Cheeks
brilliant with health & spirits, he suddenly drooped,
became pale, languid, hot & short breathed. This
continued all Day, & towards evening increased into a
restlessness that soon became misery – he refused any
food – his Eyes became red, dull, & heavy, his breath
feverish, & his limbs in almost convulsive tribulation ...
The spots began to appear, but yet Tuesday also was
very suffering – however, I will not go on with this
triste journal, but tell my dearest dear Susan that *now*
all is deliciously well! They began to turn yesterday, &
this Day, which makes but the fortnight from the
operation, many of them are already fading away, –
his appetite is returned, his gaiety is revived, all fever is
over, & if his face was not changed, the disorder would
not be suspected. I know how you will feel for our
excessive joy at this conquest of a dread that has hung
cruelly over our best happiness. We have been so much
frightened, that we would have compromised with fate
for the loss of all his personal recommendation, to
have ensured his life. ... He will be but slightly, if at
all, marked, though he has more than he will yet let me
count of these frightful boutons. Only one, however,
has risen in order; the rest come up half way, & seem
dying off for want of nourishment: Mr A. says this is
the recompence of his state of blood. He has 13 upon
his Face; 3 upon his Nose, in particular, which disfigure
it most comically. They give him, his Father says, the
air d'un petit Ivrogne ...

Like Fanny Burney, Mary Wollstonecraft was already an established writer before she began to bear children. She was thirty-five when her daughter Fanny was born in revolutionary France, fathered by an American to whom Mary was not married because they both disapproved of the institution. Mary considered that her own upbringing by a dissolute father and weak-willed mother had been cruel, and wished to raise her children on rational and affectionate principles. The little lessons she wrote for Fanny were published after Mary's death in 1797, following the birth of her second child.

Mary Wollstonecraft to her friend Ruth Barlow, 20 May 1794

Le Havre

Here I am, my Dear Friend, and so well, that were it not for the inundation of milk, which for the moment incommodes me, I could forget the pain I endured six days ago. – Yet nothing could be more natural or easy than my labour – still it is not smooth work – I dwell on these circumstances not only as I know it will give you pleasure; but to prove that this struggle of nature is rendered much more cruel by the ignorance and affectation of women. My nurse has been twenty years in this employment, and she tells me, she never knew a woman so well – adding, Frenchwoman like, that I ought to make children for the Republic, since I treat it so slightly – It is true, at first, she was convinced that I should kill myself and my child; but since we are alive and so astonishingly well, she begins to think that the *Bon Dieu* takes care of those who take no care of themselves. ... I feel great pleasure at being a mother. ...

LESSON VII

When you were hungry, you began to cry, because you could not speak. You were seven months without

[34]

teeth, always sucking. But after you got one, you began to gnaw a crust of bread. It was not long before another came pop. At ten months you had four pretty white teeth, and you used to bite me. Poor mamma! Still I did not cry, because I am not a child, but you hurt me very much. So I said to papa, it is time the little girl should eat. She is not naughty, yet she hurts me. I have given her a crust of bread, and I must look for some other milk.

The cow has got plenty, and her jumping calf eats grass very well. He has got more teeth than my little girl. Yes, says papa, and he tapped you on the cheek, you are old enough to learn to eat? Come to me, and I will teach you, my little dear, for you must not hurt poor mamma, who has given you her milk, when you could not take anything else.

LESSON VIII

You were then on the carpet, for you could not walk well. So when you were in a hurry, you used to run quick, quick, quick, on your hands and feet, like the dog.

Away you ran to papa, and putting both your arms round his leg, for your hands were not big enough, you looked up at him, and laughed. What did this laugh say, when you could not speak? Cannot you guess by what you now say to papa? – Ah! it was, Play with me, papa! – play with me!

Papa began to smile, and you knew that the smile was always – Yes. So you got a ball, and papa threw it along the floor – Roll – roll – roll; and you ran after it again – and again. How pleased you were. Look at William, he smiles; but you could laugh loud – Ha! ha! ha! – Papa laughed louder than the little girl, and rolled the ball still faster.

LESSON X

See how much taller you are than William. In four years you have learned to eat, to walk, to talk. Why do you smile? You can do much more, you think: you can wash your hands and face. Very well. I should never kiss a dirty face. And you can comb your head with a pretty comb you always put by in your drawer. To be sure, you do all this to be ready to take a walk with me. You would be obliged to stay at home, if you could not comb your own hair. Betty is busy getting the dinner ready, and only brushes William's hair, because he cannot do it for himself.

Betty is making an apple-pye. You love an apple-pye; but I do not bid you make one. Your hands are not strong enough to mix the butter and flour together; and you must not try to pare the apples, because you cannot manage the great knife.

Never touch the large knives: they are very sharp, and you might cut your finger to the bone. You are a little girl, and ought to have a little knife. When you are as tall as I am, you shall have a knife as large as mine; and when you are as strong as I am, and have learned to manage it, you will not hurt yourself.

You can trundle a hoop, you say; and jump over a stick. O, I forgot! – and march like the men in the red coats, when papa plays a pretty tune on the fiddle.

Maria Edgeworth acted as surrogate mother to her three successive stepmothers' children, and as her father's chief assistant in educating them. These anecdotes are taken from Practical Education, *of which they were co-authors, published in 1798.*

The simple language of childhood has been preserved without alteration in the following notes; and as we could not devise any better arrangement, we have followed the order of time, and we have constantly inserted the ages of the children, for the satisfaction of preceptors and parents, to whom alone these infantine anecdotes can be interesting. We say nothing farther as to their accuracy; if the reader does not see in the anecdotes themselves internal marks of veracity, all we could say would be of no avail.

X – (a girl of five years old) asked why a piece of paper fell quickly to the ground when rumpled up, but so slowly when opened.

Y – (a girl of three years and a half old) seeing her sister taken care of and nursed when she had chilblains, said, that she wished to have chilblains.

Z – (a girl between two and three) when her mother was putting on her bonnet, and when she was going out to walk, looked at the cat, and said with a plaintive voice, 'Poor Pussey! You have no bonnet, Pussey!'

X – (5 years old) asked why she was as tall as the trees when she was far from them.

Z – (4 years old) went to church, and when she was there said, 'Do those mens do everything better than we? because they talk so loud, and I think they read.' It was a country church, and people sang; but the child said, 'She thought they didn't sing, but roared, because they were shut up in that place, and didn't like it.'

Z – (5), meddling with a fly, said, 'she did not hurt it'. 'Were you ever a fly?' said her mother. 'Not *that I know of*', answered the child.

These prose extracts are taken from Coleridge's notebooks, in which his descriptions of his children have a precise, scientific air. In the poem, written in February 1798, he is more inclined to project his own dissatisfactions and hopes on his infant son.

1797

... Children in the wind – hair floating, tossing, a miniature of the agitated Trees, below which they play'd – the elder whirling for joy, the one in petticoats, a fat Baby, eddying half willingly, half by force of the Gust – driven backward, struggling forward – both drunk with the pleasure, both shouting their hymn of Joy.

1803

July 6th

Derwent to whom I was explaining what his senses were for – he had never once thought of connecting sight with his eyes, &c – I asked him what his Tongue was for & I told him/& to convince, held his Tongue/ he was not at all affected – having been used to have his voluntary power controlled by others. Sometime after I asked him again/he had forgotten – I bade him hold his Tongue and try to say, Papa – he did, & finding that he could not speak, he turned pale as death and in the reaction from fear flushed red, & gave me a blow in the face/ 2 years & 10 months old, within 8 days.

Sunday July 10th

Derwent fever-hot. The Day before he ran round & round in the kitchen so long that for the first time in his consciousness he became giddy – he turned pale with fright, & repeatedly cried – 'the kissen is walking away from Derwent' – pawing out his hands as if stopping it.

FROST AT MIDNIGHT

The Frost performs its secret ministry,
Unhelped by any wind. The owlet's cry
Came loud – and hark, again! loud as before.
The inmates of my cottage, all at rest,
Have left me to that solitude, which suits
Abstruser musings: save that at my side
My cradled infant slumbers peacefully.
'Tis calm indeed! so calm, that it disturbs
And vexes meditation with its strange
And extreme silentness. Sea, hill, and wood,
This populous village! Sea, and hill, and wood,
With all the numberless goings-on of life,
Inaudible as dreams! the thin blue flame
Lies on my low-burnt fire, and quivers not;
Only that film, which fluttered on the grate,
Still flutters there, the sole unquiet thing.
Methinks, its motion in this hush of nature
Gives it dim sympathies with me who live,
Making it a companionable form,
Whose puny flaps and freaks the idling Spirit
By its own moods interprets, every where
Echo or mirror seeking of itself,
And makes a toy of Thought.

                      But O! how oft,
How oft, at school, with most believing mind,
Presageful, have I gazed upon the bars,
To watch that fluttering *stranger!* and as oft
  With unclosed lids, already had I dreamt
Of my sweet birth-place, and the old church-tower,
Whose bells, the poor man's only music, rang
From morn to evening, all the hot Fair-day,
So sweetly, that they stirred and haunted me
With a wild pleasure, falling on mine ear
Most like articulate sounds of things to come!

So gazed I, till the soothing things, I dreamt,
Lulled me to sleep, and sleep prolonged my dreams!
And so I brooded all the following morn,
Awed by the stern preceptor's face, mine eye
Fixed with mock study on my swimming book:
Save if the door half opened, and I snatched
A hasty glance, and still my heart leaped up,
For still I hoped to see the *stranger's* face,
Townsman, or aunt, or sister more beloved,
My play-mate when we both were clothed alike!

Dear Babe, that sleepest cradled by my side,
Whose gentle breathings, heard in this deep calm,
Fill up the interspersed vacancies
And momentary pauses of the thought!
My babe so beautiful! it thrills my heart
With tender gladness, thus to look at thee,
And think that thou shalt learn far other lore,
And in far other scenes! For I was reared
In the great city, pent 'mid cloisters dim,
And saw nought lovely but the sky and stars.
But *thou*, my babe! shalt wander like a breeze
By lakes and sandy shores, beneath the crags
Of ancient mountain, and beneath the clouds,
Which image in their bulk both lakes and shores
And mountain crags: so shalt thou see and hear
The lovely shapes and sounds intelligible
Of that eternal language, which thy God
Utters, who from eternity doth teach
Himself in all, and all things in himself.
Great universal Teacher! he shall mould
Thy spirit, and by giving make it ask.

Therefore all seasons shall be sweet to thee,
Whether the summer clothe the general earth
With greenness, or the redbreast sit and sing
Betwixt the tufts of snow on the bare branch

Of mossy apple-tree, while the nigh thatch
Smokes in the sun-thaw; whether the eave-drops fall
Heard only in the trances of the blast,
Or if the secret ministry of frost
Shall hang them up in silent icicles,
Quietly shining to the quiet Moon.

William Godwin's humanist paeon to a newborn child is almost ecstatic. The emotional weight is becoming very great; possibly parents and children are expecting too much of one another. Storms will follow.

Never shall I forget the interview between us immediately subsequent to her first parturition, the effusion with which we met each other after all danger seemed to have subsided, the kindness which animated us, increased as it was by the ideas of peril and suffering, the sacred sensation with which the mother presented her infant to her husband, or the complacency with which we read in each other's eyes a common sentiment of melting tenderness and inviolable attachment!

This, she seemed to say, is the joint result of our common affection. It partakes equally of both, and is the shrine in which our sympathies and our life have been poured together, by presents and tokens; we record and stamp our attachment in this precious creature, a creature of that species which is more admirable than anything else the world has to boast, a creature susceptible of pleasure and pain, of affection and love, of sentiment and fancy, of wisdom and virtue. This creature will daily stand in need of an aid we shall delight to afford; will require our meditations and exertions to forward its improvement, and confirm its merits and its worth. We shall each blend our exertions for the purpose, and our union confirmed by this common object of our labour and affection, will every day become more sacred and indissoluble.

From *St Leon,* 1799

Here is Percy Bysshe Shelley writing to his sixty-year-old father, from York, 12 October 1811, after some unavailing requests for funds. Shelley is just twenty, has quarrelled with his father, first by refusing to accept the doctrines of Christianity and secondly over his runaway marriage with a schoolgirl of sixteen.

Dear Father

The waggoner has written to inform me that my property is sent – but does it not look as if your resentment was not to be supported by reason that you have declined to write yourself?

I cannot avoid thinking thus, nor expressing my opinion; but silence, especially on so important a subject as I urged, looks as if you confessed the erroneousness of your proceedings, at the same time that your passions impel you to persist in them. I do not say this is illiberal, a person who can once persuade himself as you have done that every opinion adopted by the majority is correct, must be nearly indifferent to this charge; I do not say it is immoral, as illiberality involves a portion of immorality, but it is emphatically hostile to your own interest, to the opinion which the world will form of your virtues. *If* you are a professor of Christianity, which I am not, I need not recall to your recollection 'Judge not lest thou shouldst be judged'.

I confess I write this more to discharge a duty of telling you what I think, than hoping that my representations will be effectual. We have taken widely different views of the subject in question. *Obedience* is in my opinion a word which should have no existence – you regard it as necessary. –

Yes, you can command it. The institutions of society have made you, tho' liable to be misled by passion and prejudice like others, the *Head of the family*; and I confess it is almost natural for minds not of the highest order to value even the errors whence they derive their importance.

Adieu, answer this. –

I would be your aff. dut. Son
Percy B. Shelley

The Autobiography of Elizabeth Fletcher *was published in 1875 but written in July 1817. An appendix describes the death of Mrs Fletcher's twenty-one-year-old daughter Grace.*

On Friday morning she sent for me, and said, 'Oh, mamma, I have had a dreadful night, but I think I could sleep in your arms.' I laid myself down beside her. She said, 'Let us pray'; and she slowly and distinctly repeated the Lord's Prayer. She then laid her head on my breast, and seemed to sleep quietly for a few minutes. On raising her head again, she said, 'Dearest mother, I have had my first sleep where I had my first food.' Soon afterwards there was an increase of heat and headache, which was not removed by the application of more leeches to the temples. During the whole of the day (Friday) her restlessness and anxiety increased, and towards night high delirium came on. . . .

On Tuesday Dr Thomson thought her decidedly better. On that night, when I was sitting by her bedside, she said – 'Bring a candle, and let the light shine full on mamma's face, that I may see her.' When the candle was brought, she fixed her eyes on me with an expression of tender earnestness for a few minutes, as if to search my thoughts, or, perhaps, to look her last. At this time she seemed not to recognise any of the rest who attended her; but whenever I approached her bed she stretched out her arms, and once she said – 'Dearest mother, if I should die, I do not suffer excessive pain.'

After another week of suffering, delirium and prayer, Grace became unable to take even the wine the doctor ordered.

. . . All hope was now over. She passed a day of great suffering from sickness, and there was no interruption to the delirium; but her voice was strong, and I was not aware that all would so soon be over. 'Mamma, mamma,' were the last words she uttered.

She died on Wednesday night, at ten o'clock, April 16th 1817. . . . Never was there such tender, dutiful, fond, and respectful affection as her whole short life exemplified. Thankful to God for having given me such a child, and still for sparing me so many blessings in those that remain, may we be enabled so to live that, when time shall be no more, we may be reunited to her in a blessed immortality.

ELIZA WEETON

Eliza Weeton was orphaned early, had to earn her living as a governess and then made a wretchedly unhappy marriage; but she set down her life of obscurity and misfortune with a spirited, feminist pen, and she obviously took special note of her father's remark about daughters and their fate.

My father was for some time captain of a merchantman in the African slave trade, but the American war breaking out, he was next commissioned ... to command a vessel carrying a Letter of Marque [i.e., permission to attack enemy vessels and win prize money]. In this vessel he sailed, and in the course of his voyage took many prizes. He returned, and was loaded with congratulations for his successful bravery. During this period, my mother had brought him three children; Edward, the eldest, who died at $3\frac{1}{2}$ years old; next myself, born on Christmas Day, 1776, and christened by the name of Nelly. My father being out on a voyage when I was born, my mother was at a loss what name to give me; but knowing that the ship Nelly in which he was sailing, was a great favourite of his, she thought to win his affection for me by naming me after it, as she had heard him say that he could wish his children to be all boys. When he returned, and she told him this, he expressed himself as very sorry that she should have been hurt by what he said; declaring that he loved me as much as Edward (who was only 11 months older than I); but, he said, unless a father can provide independent fortunes for his daughters, they must either be mop squeezers, or mantua makers, whereas sons can easily make their way in the world.

From *The Journal of Eliza Weeton*, 1824

Relations between Charles Dickens and his parents were not good, especially after his mother urged that he should continue to work in a blacking factory rather than return to school after his father's release from debtors' prison. Charles was twelve at the time: 'I never afterwards forgot, I never shall forget, I never can forget that my mother was warm for my being sent back.' He gave a very different mother to his semi-autobiographical David Copperfield, *which appeared in 1849–50. The gentle and childlike Clara, crushed by childbearing and a cruel husband, becomes the perfect image of a lost, ideal mother; and on her unhappy deathbed she blesses her young son 'not once, but a thousand times', as David's old nurse Peggotty tells him.*

From the moment of my knowing of the death of my mother, the idea of her as she had been of late had vanished from me. I remembered her, from that instant, only as the young mother of my earliest impressions, who had been used to wind her bright curls round and round her finger, and to dance with me at twilight in the parlour. What Peggotty had told me now, was so far from bringing me back to the later period, that it rooted the earlier image in my mind. It may be curious, but it is true. In her death she winged her way back to her calm untroubled youth, and cancelled all the rest.

The mother who lay in the grave, was the mother of my infancy; the little creature in her arms, was myself, as I had once been, hushed for ever on her bosom.

Elizabeth Gaskell was not given to self-revelation, but this poem and the few phrases from her letters suggest that her maternal feelings were particularly intense.

ELIZABETH GASKELL

ON VISITING THE GRAVE OF
MY STILLBORN LITTLE GIRL

Sunday, July 4th, 1836

I made a vow within my soul, O child,
When thou wert laid beside my weary heart,
With marks of death on every tender part,
That, if in time a living infant smiled,
Winning my ear with gentle sounds of love
In sunshine of such joy, I still would save
A green rest for thy memory, O Dove!
And oft times visit thy small, nameless grave.
Thee have I not forgot, my firstborn, thou
Whose eyes ne'er opened to my wistful gaze,
Whose sufferings tamped with pain thy little brow;
I think of thee in these far happier days,
And thou, my child, from thy bright heaven see
How well I keep my faithful vow to thee.

I have just been up to our room. There is a fire in it, and a smell of baking, and oddly enough the feelings and recollections of three years ago came over me so strongly – when I used to sit up in the room so often in the evenings reading by the fire, and watching my darling *darling* Willie, who now sleeps sounder still in the dull, dreary chapel-yard at Warrington. That wound will never heal on earth, although hardly any one knows how it has changed me. I wish you had seen my little fellow, dearest dear Annie. I can give you no idea what a darling he was – so affectionate and *reasonable* a baby I never saw. . . .

From a letter to Anne Shaen, written in April 1848

I think she has passed the acme of her life, – when all is over and the little first born darling lies nuzzling and cooing by one's side. . . .

From a letter of 1863 to Charles Norton,
whose wife had just given birth

Alfred Tennyson's first-born 'grand massive manchild' was strangled by the umbilical cord during the birth, in 1815. Tennyson wrote:

It was Easter Sunday and at his birth I heard the great roll of the organ, of the uplifted psalm (in the Chapel adjoining the house). . . . Dead as he was I felt proud of him. Today when I write this down, the remembrance of it rather overcomes me; but I am glad that I have seen him, dear little nameless one that hast lived tho' thou has never breathed, I, thy father, love thee and weep over thee, tho' thou hast no place in the Universe. Who knows? It may be that thou hast . . . God's Will be done.

Anny Thackeray, the daughter of the novelist, was born in 1837; early in her parents' marriage her mother lapsed into madness and lived apart from the family. Anny and her younger sister Minny were brought up by their father and grandparents. Here Anny is fourteen, Minny eleven.

I suppose the outer circuit of my own very limited wanderings must have been reached at the age of

thirteen or thereabouts, when my father took me and
my little sister for the grand tour of Europe. We had, of
course, lived in Paris and spent our summers in quiet
country places abroad with our grandparents, but this
was to be something different from anything we had
ever known before at St. Germains or Montmorenci
among the donkeys; Switzerland, and Venice, and
Vienna, Germany and the Rhine! Our young souls
thrilled with expectation. And yet those early feasts of
life are not unlike the miracle of the loaves and the
fishes; the twelve basketfuls that remain in after years
are certainly even more precious than the feast itself.

We started one sleety summer morning. My father
was pleased to be off, and we were enchanted. He had
brought a gray wide-awake hat for the journey, and he
had a new sketch book in his pocket, besides two
smaller ones for us, which he produced as the steamer
was starting. We sailed from London Bridge, and the
decks were all wet and slippery as we came on board.
We were scatter-brained little girls, although we looked
demure enough in our mushroom hats and waterproofs.
We also had prepared a travelling trousseau ... which
consisted I remember of a draught board, a large
wooden work-box, a good many books, paint boxes,
and other odds and ends: but I felt that whatever else
might be deficient our *new bonnets* would bring us
triumphantly out of every crisis. They were alike, but
with a difference of blue and pink wreaths of acacia,
and brilliant in ribbons to match, at a time when people
affected less dazzling colours than they do now. Alas!
for human expectations! When the happy moment
came at last, and we had reached foreign parts and
issued out of the hotel dressed and wreathed and
triumphantly splendid, my father said 'My dear
children go back and put those bonnets away in your
box, and don't ever wear them any more!' How the sun

shone as he spoke; how my heart sank under the acacia trees. My sister was eleven years old, and didn't care a bit; but at thirteen and fourteen one's clothes begin to strike root. I felt disgraced, beheaded of my lovely bonnet, utterly crushed, and I turned away to hide my tears.

From *Chapters from Some Memoirs*, 1894

Tom Brown's Schooldays, by Thomas Hughes, was published in 1857 but set in the 1830s. Tom never questions his father's 'strength and courage and wisdom' any more than his mother's 'love, tenderness and purity'. The book was still selling in cheap editions in 1914. Here Squire Brown wonders what to tell his son Tom as he goes off to school.

'I won't tell him to read his Bible, and love and serve God; if he don't do that for his mother's sake and teaching, he won't for mine. Shall I go into the sort of temptations he'll meet with? No, I can't do that. Never do for an old fellow to go into such things with a boy. He won't understand me. Do him more harm than good, ten to one. Shall I tell him to mind his work, and say he's sent to school to make himself a good scholar? Well, but he isn't sent to school for that – at any rate, not for that mainly. I don't care a straw for Greek particles, or the digamma; no more does his mother. What is he sent to school for? Well, partly because he wanted to go. If he'll only turn out a brave, helpful, truth-telling Englishman, and a gentleman and a Christian, that's all I want', thought the Squire.

Maggie Tulliver, a small girl in a temper, has cut off most of her hair and now appears at the family dinner table.

Mrs Tulliver's scream made all eyes turn towards the same point as her own, and Maggie's cheeks and ears began to burn, while uncle Glegg, a kind-looking, white-haired old gentleman, said –

'Hey-day! what little gell's this – why, I don't know her. Is it some little gell you've picked up in the road, Kezia?'

'Why, she's gone and cut her hair herself,' said Mr Tulliver in an undertone to Mr Deane, laughing with much enjoyment. 'Did you ever know such a little hussy as it is?'

'Why, little miss, you've made yourself look very funny,' said uncle Pullet, and perhaps he never in his life made an observation which was felt to be so lacerating.

'Fie, for shame!' said aunt Glegg in her loudest, severest tone of reproof. 'Little gells as cut their own hair should be whipped and fed on bread and water – not come and sit down with their aunts and uncles.'

'Ay, ay,' said uncle Glegg, meaning to give a playful turn to this denunciation, 'she must be sent to jail, I think, and they'll cut the rest of her hair off there, and make it all even.'

'She's more like a gypsy nor ever,' said aunt Pullet, in a pitying tone; 'it's very bad luck, sister, as the gell should be so brown – the boy's fair enough. I doubt it'll stand in her way i'life, to be so brown.'

'She's a naughty child, as'll break her mother's heart,' said Mrs Tulliver, with the tears in her eyes.

Maggie seemed to be listening to a chorus of reproach and derision. Her first flush came from anger, which gave her a transient power of defiance, and Tom thought she was braving it out, supported by the recent appearance of the pudding and custard. Under this impression he whispered, 'O my! Maggie, I told you you'd catch it.' He meant to be friendly, but Maggie felt convinced that Tom was rejoicing in her ignominy. Her feeble power of defiance left her in an instant, her heart swelled, and, getting up from her chair, she ran to her father, hid her face on his shoulder, and burst out into loud sobbing.

'Come, come, my wench,' said her father, soothingly, putting his arm round her, 'never mind; you was i'the right to cut it off if it plagued you; give over crying: father'll take your part.'

Delicious words of tenderness! Maggie never forgot any of these moments when her father 'took her part'; she kept them in her heart, and thought of them long years after, when everyone else said that her father had done very ill by his children.

George Eliot, *The Mill on the Floss*, 1860

Samuel Butler wrote The Way of All Flesh *in the 1870s, but it was not published until a year after his death, in 1903. Ernest is of course Butler himself, and the whole book is his indictment of the Victorian rectory upbringing he received.*

I was there on a Sunday, and observed the rigour with which the young people were taught to observe the Sabbath: they might not cut out things, nor use their paint box on a Sunday, and this they thought rather hard because their cousins the John Pontifexes might do these things. Their cousins might play with their toy train on Sunday, but though they had promised that they would run none but Sunday trains, all traffic had been prohibited. One treat only was allowed them – on Sunday evenings they might choose their own hymns.

In the course of the evening they came into the drawing-room and as an especial treat were to sing some of their hymns to me instead of saying them, so that I might hear how nicely they sang. Ernest was to choose the first hymn and he chose one about some people who were to come to the sunset tree. I am no botanist, and do not know what kind of a tree a sunset tree is, but the words began, 'Come, come, come; come to the sunset tree for the day is past and gone.' The tune was rather pretty and had taken Ernest's fancy, for he was unusually fond of music and had a sweet little child's voice which he liked using.

He was, however, very late in being able to sound a hard C or K, and instead of saying 'Come,' he said 'tum, tum, tum.'

'Ernest,' said Theobald from the armchair in front of the fire where he was sitting with his hands folded before him, 'don't you think it would be very nice if you were to say "come" like other people, instead of "tum"?'

'I do say tum,' replied Ernest, meaning that he had said 'come.'

Theobald was always in a bad temper on Sunday evening. Whether it is that they are as much bored with the day as their neighbours, or whether they are tired, or whatever the cause may be, clergymen are seldom at their best on Sunday evening; I had already seen signs that evening that my host was cross, and was a little nervous at hearing Ernest say so promptly, 'I do say tum,' when his papa had said he did not say it as he should.

Theobald noticed the fact that he was being contradicted in a moment. He had been sitting in an armchair in front of the fire with his hands folded, doing nothing, but he got up at once and went to the piano.

'No Ernest, you don't,' he said; 'you say nothing of the kind, you say "tum" not "come." Now say "come" after me, as I do.'

'Tum,' said Ernest at once, 'is that better?' I have no doubt he thought it was, but it was not.

'Now Ernest, you are not taking pains: you are not trying as you ought to do. It is high time you learned to say "come"; why Joey can say "come," can't you, Joey?'

'Yeth I can,' replied Joey promptly, and he said something which was not far off 'come'.

'There, Ernest, do you hear that? There's no difficulty about it nor shadow of difficulty. Now take your own time; think about it and say "come" after me.

The boy remained silent for a few seconds and then said 'tum' again.

I laughed, but Theobald turned to me impatiently and said, 'Please do not laugh Overton, it will make the boy think it does not matter, and it matters a great deal'; then turning to Ernest he said, 'Now Ernest, I will give you one more chance, and if you don't say "come" I shall know that you are self-willed and naughty.'

He looked very angry and a shade came over Ernest's face, like that which comes upon the face of a puppy when it is being scolded without understanding why. The child saw well what was coming now, was frightened, and of course said 'tum' once more.

'Very well Ernest,' said his father catching him angrily by the shoulder. 'I have done my best to save you but if you will have it so you will,' and he lugged the little wretch out of the room crying by anticipation. A few minutes more and we could hear screams coming from the dining-room across the hall which separated the drawing-room from the dining-room, and knew that poor Ernest was being beaten.

'I have sent him up to bed,' said Theobald, as he returned to the drawing-room, 'and now, Christina, I think we will have the servants in to prayers,' and he rang the bell for them, red-handed as he was.

COVENTRY PATMORE

THE TOYS

My little Son, who looked from thoughtful eyes,
And moved and spoke in quiet grown-up wise,
Having my law the seventh time disobeyed,
I struck him, and dismissed
With hard words and unkissed,
– His Mother, who was patient, being dead.
Then, fearing lest his grief should hinder sleep,
I visited his bed,
But found him slumbering deep,
With darkened eyelids, and their lashes yet
From his late sobbing wet.
And I, with moan,
Kissing away his tears, left others of my own;
For on a table drawn beside his head,
He had put, within his reach,
A box of counters and a red-veined stone,
A piece of glass abraded by the beach,
And six or seven shells,
A bottle with bluebells,
And two French copper coins, ranged there with
    careful art,
To comfort his sad heart.
So when that night I prayed
To God, I wept, and said:
Ah, when at last we lie with trancéd breath,
Not vexing Thee in death,
And Thou rememberest of what toys
We made our joys,
How weakly understood
Thy great commanded good,
Then fatherly not less
Than I whom Thou has moulded from the clay,
Thou'lt leave Thy wrath, and say,
'I will be sorry for their childishness.'

Coventry Patmore (1823–96)

[55]

Edmund Gosse was born in 1849; his mother died in 1857.

It was not ... until the course of my seventh year
that the tragedy occurred, which altered the whole
course of our family existence. My Mother had hitherto
seemed strong and in good health; she even made the
remark to my Father, that 'sorrow and pain, the badges
of Christian discipleship', appeared to be withheld
from her. ... But a symptom began to alarm her, and
in the beginning of May, having consulted a physician
without being satisfied, she went to see a specialist in a
northern suburb in whose judgement she had great
confidence. This occasion I recollect with extreme
vividness. I had been put to bed by my Father, in itself
a noteworthy event. My crib stood near a window over-
looking the street; my parents' ancient four-poster, a
relic of the eighteenth century, hid me from the door,
but I could see the rest of the room. After falling asleep
on this particular evening, I awoke silently, surprised to
see two lighted candles on the table, and my Father
seated writing by them. I also saw a little meal arranged.

While I was wondering at all this, the door opened,
and my Mother entered the room; she emerged from
behind the bed-curtains, with her bonnet on, having
returned from her expedition. My Father rose hur-
riedly, pushing back his chair. There was a pause,
while my Mother seemed to be steadying her voice,
and then she replied, loudly and distinctly, 'He says it
is – ' and she mentioned one of the most cruel maladies
by which our poor mortal nature can be tormented.
Then I saw them fold one another in a long silent
embrace, and presently sink together out of sight on
their knees, at the farther side of the bed, whereupon
my Father lifted up his voice in prayer. Neither of
them had noticed me, and now I lay back on my
pillow and fell asleep.

Next morning, when we three sat at breakfast, my

mind reverted to the scene of the previous night. With my eyes on my plate, as I was cutting up my food, I asked, casually, 'What is – ?' mentioning the disease whose unfamiliar name I had heard from my bed. Receiving no reply, I looked up to discover why my question was not answered, and I saw my parents gazing at each other with lamentable eyes. In some way, I know not how, I was conscious of the presence of an incommunicable mystery, and I kept silence, though tortured with curiosity, nor did I ever repeat my inquiry. . . .

Now, and for the first time in my life, I no longer slept in her room, no longer sank to sleep under her kiss, no longer saw her mild eyes smile on me with the earliest sunshine. Twice a day, after breakfast and before I went to rest, I was brought to her bedside; but we were never alone, other people, sometimes strange people, were there. We had no cosy talk; often she was too weak to do more than pat my hand; her loud and almost constant cough terrified and harassed me. I felt, as I stood, awkwardly and shyly, by her high bed, that I had shrunken into a very small and insignificant figure, that she was floating out of my reach, that all things, but I knew not what nor how, were coming to an end.

. . . in memory, my childhood was long, long with interminable hours, hours with the pale cheek pressed against the window-pane, hours of mechanical and repeated lonely 'games', which had lost their savour, and were kept going by sheer inertness. Not unhappy, not fretful, but long, – long, long. It seems to me, as I look back to the life in my motherless Islington house, as I resumed it in that slow eighth year of my life, that time had ceased to move. There was a whole age between one tick of the eight-day clock in the hall, and the next tick. When the milkman went his rounds in our grey street, with his eldritch scream over the top of each set of area railings, it seemed as though he would never disappear again. There was no past and no future for me, and the present felt as though it were sealed up in a Leyden jar. Even my dreams were interminable, and hung stationary from the nightly sky.

From *Father and Son*, 1907

MATER TRIUMPHANS

Son of my woman's body, you go, to the drum and fife,
To taste the colour of love and the other side of life –
From out of the dainty the rude, the strong from out of
    the frail,
Eternally through the ages from the female comes the
    male.

The ten fingers and toes, and the shell-like nail on
    each,
The eyes blind as gems and the tongue attempting
    speech;
Impotent hands in my bosom, and yet they shall
    wield the sword!
Drugged with slumber and milk, you wait the day of
    the Lord.

Infant bridegroom, uncrowned king, unanointed
   priest,
Soldier, lover, explorer, I see you nuzzle the breast.
You that grope in my bosom shall load the ladies with
   rings,
You, that came forth through the doors, shall burst the
   doors of kings.

                            Robert Louis Stevenson (1850–94)

My father's sister Laura ... had as a girl a sad and
lonely life, which fortunately did not quench her
natural vivacity. She was sent to a school for the
daughters of officers and returned without pleasure to
Chesterfield Street for the holidays, since she had to
face being snubbed, ignored, humiliated or ordered
about by her mother. Instances of mutual animosity
between mother and daughter are not rare. . . It is as
if each saw in the other a rival. To call such a relationship unnatural is not reasonable, since we naturally
tend to hate those whom, even if it be only in one
particular trait, we most resemble. . . .

Laura found that only one thing was expected of
her – to marry as soon as possible a man with money,
of at least her own but preferably of a higher social
status, and her obligation to do this was dinned into her
unceasingly. Prospective suitors seem to have appeared
on the scene when she was still remarkably young – she
was pretty and sprightly and evidently not without
fortune – and since they received every encourage-
ment from her mother, Laura delighted in turning
them down, even though her firmness led to stormy
scenes. In due course she saw her chance of escape and
happiness and decided to take it. Her mother sometimes allowed her to go and stay in other people's
houses, being glad to get her out of her sight and hoping
she might fall in with a suitable *parti*, and in one of

these absences her meeting with a certain young man duly kindled what would once have been described as a mutual flame. He was the only son of a family of rich Quaker merchants, had been educated privately, and was something of an aesthete. His name was Horniman, and the money came from that popular beverage known as Horniman's Pure Tea.

To Laura the young Horniman proposed, and by Laura he was accepted, though her parents had never set eyes on him. The fact that she had accepted him would no doubt have been enough to set her mother against the proposed match, news of which let loose all Helen's rage. She was ordered to put the matter out of her head at once and hold no further communication with the young man. . . . Laura, however, was not one of those drooping, docile Victorian daughters: she had a will of her own, and the fact that she was ordered not to speak of the young man or give him any further thought – let alone see him or communicate with him – only heightened her resolve.

The recalcitrant Laura, though by now almost grown up, was actually imprisoned in her room until she should 'come to her senses', but these were in fact exactly what she had come to. . . . The direst threat was patterned on an old formula: 'If you marry this man, we shall no longer look upon you as our daughter. You will be disgracing yourself, and we shall never wish to see you again. You will be to us exactly as if you were dead.' To which the answer was the contemporary equivalent of 'So what?' and a flurry of home truths. Finally it was obvious even to the stubborn father and bitter mother that nothing would move the girl, so they gave in, allowed her to be married from her own home, and accompanied her to St George's, Hanover Square, and back, Helen in sables and a white fury, Laura radiant with ferocious joy. . . . She went off with a new name to a new life with her radical aesthete, and enjoyed, for the next half-century or so, health, wealth, and much happiness.

Many years later ... early in the present century, when Laura was the happy mother of several children, her own mother, old and disintegrating, sought a reconciliation: she wrote and asked Laura to come and see her. Laura made no move to do so, but one afternoon, after the lapse of some weeks, she was trying on a new green velvet dress and much admiring herself in the glass, when she suddenly decided to go and see her mother. Two sentences of the conversation have been recorded.

'I wonder what your children think of me,' said the old woman, who was in bed.

'My children!' cried the unforgiving Laura, full of radiant vitality and again catching sight of her reflection and that of the green velvet dress in a glass. 'My children! Why, they don't even know that you exist!'

William Plomer, *Double Lives*, 1943

D. H. Lawrence was born in 1885, the son of a Nottingham miner and his wife. Sons and Lovers, *from which this passage is taken, was published in 1913. It is fictionalized autobiography, recreating his own infancy and boyhood and showing how his mother, finding her life emotionally and intellectually barren, sought redress through a passionate attachment to her sons.*

In her arms lay the delicate baby. Its deep blue eyes, always looking up at her unblinking, seemed to draw her innermost thoughts out of her. She no longer loved her husband; she had not wanted this child to come, and there it lay in her arms and pulled at her heart. She felt as if the navel string that had connected its frail little body with hers had not been broken. A wave of hot love went over her to the infant. She held it close to her face and breast. With all her force, with all her soul she would make up to it for having brought it into the world unloved. She would love it all the more now it was here; carry it in her love. Its clear, knowing eyes gave her pain and fear. Did it know all about her? When it lay under her heart, had it been listening then? Was there a reproach in the look? She felt the marrow melt in her bones, with fear and pain.

Lawrence's poem 'Sorrow' was written in mourning for his mother.

> Why does the thin grey strand
> Floating up from the forgotten
> Cigarette between my fingers,
> Why does it trouble me?
>
> Ah, you will understand;
> When I carried my mother downstairs,
> A few times only, at the beginning
> Of her soft-foot malady
>
> I should find, for a reprimand
> To my gaiety, a few long grey hairs
> On the breast of my coat; and one by one
> I watched them float up the dark chimney.

from A PRAYER FOR MY DAUGHTER

> Once more the storm is howling, and half hid
> Under this cradle-hood and coverlid
> My child sleeps on. There is no obstacle
> But Gregory's wood and one bare hill
> Whereby the haystack- and roof-levelling wind,
> Bred on the Atlantic, can be stayed;
> And for an hour I have walked and prayed
> Because of the great gloom that is in my mind.

I have walked and prayed for this young child an hour
And heard the sea-wind scream upon the tower,
And under the arches of the bridge, and scream
In the elms above the flooded stream;
Imagining in excited reverie
That the future years had come,
Dancing to a frenzied drum,
Out of the murderous innocence of the sea.

May she be granted beauty and yet not
Beauty to make a stranger's eye distraught,
Or hers before a looking-glass, for such,
Being made beautiful overmuch,
Consider beauty a sufficient end,
Lose natural kindness and maybe
The heart-revealing intimacy
That chooses right, and never find a friend ...

In courtesy I'd have her chiefly learned;
Hearts are not had as a gift but hearts are earned
By those that are not entirely beautiful;
Yet many, that have played the fool
For beauty's very self, has charm made wise,
And many a poor man that has roved,
Loved and thought himself beloved,
From a glad kindness cannot take his eyes.

May she become a flourishing hidden tree
That all her thoughts may like the linnet be,
And have no business but dispensing round
Their magnanimities of sound,
Nor but in merriment begin a chase,
Nor but in merriment a quarrel.
O may she live like some green laurel
Rooted in one dear perpetual place ...

Considering that, all hatred driven hence,
The soul recovers radical innocence
And learns at last that it is self-delighting,
Self-appeasing, self-affrighting,
And that its own sweet will is Heaven's will;
She can, though every face should scowl
And every windy quarter howl
Or every bellows burst, be happy still.

And may her bridegroom bring her to a house
Where all's accustomed, ceremonious;
For arrogance and hatred are the wares
Peddled in the thoroughfares.
How but in custom and in ceremony
Are innocence and beauty born?
Ceremony's a name for the rich horn,
And custom for the spreading laurel tree.

June 1919   W. B. Yeats (1865–1939)

[64]

Naomi Mitchison's account of her upbringing in a high-minded, intellectual household in North Oxford before World War I comes from her Small Talk, *published in 1973.*

I was being taught to read by my mother at home. It was a phonetic system and at four I had no bother with cat, mat and sat but suddenly I was confronted with four-letter words. A feeling overwhelmed me that I would never be able to understand, never. I have had that feeling since: about economics, about physics and, oddly, about lawn tennis. These were all things I wanted to be competent at, but felt deep down I couldn't do. Other subjects I was either good at or didn't particularly want to understand or else felt that I could if I took trouble – and sometimes did. But this dead-end feeling is unmistakable. On this first occasion it was clearly infuriating to my maternal teacher. She spanked me hard and I was put into my cot, the nursery curtains were drawn and I was left to think it over as soon as I had stopped howling. It hadn't really hurt. The offence was to my human dignity. I did not forgive it. But it made me understand how other people feel about affronted human dignity. This has been useful. It was also useful because suddenly I was able to read not only words of four letters but all words. Unhappily I never got a sufficient jolt over economics or physics.

As far as I remember my main punishment as a child was not being smacked but being told that I was 'hurting Mother'. If one was disobedient – and this was rubbed in from early readings of Kipling's *Jungle Book* which put a great emphasis on obedience as did, I think, Montefiore's *Bible for Home Reading* – or told lies or was in any way treacherous, it hurt Those who Loved One Most. Let me add that this was not a God-centred household; we were brought up as highly moral agnostics.

Magdalen Stuart Robison was born, like her husband William Pember Reeves, in New Zealand and shared his radical views. They married in 1885 and came to England when he was appointed Agent-General for the colony in 1896; in 1908 he became Director of the London School of Economics. Both he and his wife worked with the Fabian Society, and Mrs Pember Reeves's remarkable study of the family life of the poor in Lambeth and Kennington was written under its auspices.

Mr A., whose house was visited all the year of 1909, was originally a footman in one of the houses of a large public school. ... He was about 5 feet 8 inches in height, well educated, and very steady. His wife had been a lady's maid. ... Mr A. left his position as footman, and became a bus conductor in one of the old horse-bus companies. When visited in 1909 he had been fifteen years in his position, but owing to the coming of motor traffic, his employers gradually ran fewer buses, and his work became more casual. ... He had to present himself every morning, and wait a certain time before he knew whether he would be employed or not. ... His wife, who by the time the visits began was worn and delicate, was a well-educated woman, and an excellent manager. She saved on all the 20s. weeks in order to have a little extra for the 16s. weeks. ... There were five children after the baby of the investigation arrived. The eldest, a girl, was consumptive; the next, a boy, was short in one leg, and wore a surgical boot; the next, a girl, was the airless ex-baby, and suffered with its eyes; and only the newborn child, weighing 9 lb., seemed to be thriving and strong. The average per week for food was 1s. a head for man, woman and children. Presently the conductor's work stopped altogether. No more horse-buses were run on that particular route, and motor-buses did not

come that way. Mr A. was out of work. He used to
bring in odd sums of money earned in all sorts of ways
between tramping after a new job. The eldest girl was
put into a factory, where she earned 6s. a week; the
eldest boy got up early one morning, and offered himself to a dairyman as a boy to leave milk, and got the
job, which meant work from 6 a.m. till 8 a.m., and two
hours after school in the evening. Several hours on
Saturday and Sunday completed the week's work, for
which he was paid 2s. 6d. His parents were averse to
his doing this, but the boy persisted. The family
moved to basement rooms at a cheaper rent, and then
the gradual pulling down of the baby began. The
mother applied to the school authorities to have the
two boys given dinner, and after some difficulty
succeeded. The elder boy made no complaint, but the
short-legged one could not eat the meals supplied. He
said they were greasy, and made him feel sick. He
used to come home and ask for a slice of the family
bread and dripping. The father's earnings ranged
between 5s. and 10s. which brought the family income
up to anything from 13s. 6d. to 18s. 6d. The food
allowance went often as low as 8d. a week. A strain
was put upon the health of each child, which reduced
its vitality, and gave free play to disease tendencies.
The eyes, which had been a weak point in every child,
grew worse all round. The consumptive girl was
constantly at home, the boy had heavy colds, and the
younger children ailed. Work was at last found by the
father at a steady rate of 20s. a week. He took the consumptive girl from her work, and sent her into the
country, where she remained in the cottage of a grand-
parent earning nothing. The boy was induced to give
up his work, and the family, when last seen, were living
on a food allowance of 1s. 6d. per head all round the
family. The baby was the usual feeble child of her age,

the children were no longer fed at school, and the parents were congratulating themselves on their wonderful good fortune.

From *Round About a Pound a Week*, 1913

In To the Lighthouse *(1927) by Virginia Woolf, Mrs Ramsay is thinking about her children.*

Oh, but she never wanted James to grow a day older! or Cam either. These two she would have liked to keep for ever just as they were, demons of wickedness, angels of delight, never to see them grow up into long-legged monsters. Nothing made up for the loss. When she read just now to James, 'and there were numbers of soldiers with kettledrums and trumpets', and his eyes darkened, she thought, why should they grow up, and lose all that? He was the most gifted, the most sensitive of her children. But all, she thought, were full of promise. . . . Why, she asked, pressing her chin on James's head, should they grow up so fast? Why should they go to school? She would have liked always to have had a baby. . . . And, touching his hair with her lips, she thought, he will never be so happy again, but stopped herself, remembering how it angered her husband that she should say that. Still, it was true. They were happier now than they would ever be again. . . . She heard them stamping and crowing on the floor above her head the moment they woke. They came bustling along the passage. Then the door sprang open and in they came, fresh as roses, staring, wide awake, as if this coming into the dining-room after breakfast, which they did every day of their lives, was a positive event to them, and so on, with one thing after another, all day long, until she went up to say good-night to them, and found them netted in their cots like birds among cherries and raspberries, still

making up stories about some little bit of rubbish –
something they had heard, something they had picked
up in the garden. . . . And so she went down and said to
her husband, Why must they grow up and lose it all?
Never will they be so happy again. And he was angry.
Why take such a gloomy view of life? he said. It is not
sensible. . . for the most part, oddly enough, she must
admit that she felt this thing called life terrible,
hostile, and quick to pounce on you if you gave it a
chance. There were the eternal problems: suffering;
death; the poor. There was always a woman dying of
cancer even here. And yet she had said to all these
children, You shall go through it all. . . . For that
reason, knowing what was before them – love and
ambition and being wretched alone in dreary places –
she had often the feeling, Why must they grow up and
lose it all? And then she said to herself, brandishing
her sword at life, Nonsense. They will be perfectly
happy. . . . she was driven on, too quickly she knew,
almost as if it were an escape for her too, to say that
people must marry; people must have children.

*Graham Greene was born in 1904, the son of a headmaster.
This passage comes from his memoir,* A Sort of Life
(1971).

I think that my parents' was a very loving marriage;
how far any marriage is happy is another matter and
beyond an outsider's knowledge. Happiness can be
ruined by children, by financial anxieties, by so many
secret things: love too can be ruined, but I think their
love withstood the pressure of six children and great
anxieties. I was in Sierra Leone, running ineffectually a
one-man office of the Secret Service, when my father
died in 1942. The news came in two telegrams delivered
in the wrong order – the first told me of his death – the
second an hour later of his serious illness. Suddenly,
between the secret reports to be coded and decoded,
I unexpectedly felt misery and remorse, remembering
how as a young man I had deliberately set out to
shock his ideas which had been unflinchingly liberal in
politics and gently conservative in morals. I had a
Mass said for him by Father Mackey, the Irish priest
in Freetown. I thought that if my father could know he
would regard the gesture with his accustomed liberality
and kindly amusement – he had never disputed by so
much as a word my decision to become a Catholic. At
least I felt sure that my method of payment would have
pleased him. The priest asked me for a sack of rice for
his poor African parishioners, for rice was scarce and
severely rationed, and through my friendship with the
Commissioner of Police I was able to buy one clandes-
tinely.

Both parents have known someone the children
have never known. My father had known the tall girl
with the tiny waist wearing a boater, and my mother
the young dandyish man who appeared in a tinted
Oxford photograph on their bathroom wall, with a well-

trimmed moustache, wearing evening dress with a blue waistcoat. More than ten years after his death my mother wrote to me. She had broken her hip and she had dreamt unhappily that my father had not come to see her in hospital or even written to her and she couldn't understand it. Now, even when she was awake, she felt unhappy because of his silence. Oddly enough I too had dreamt of him a few days before. My mother and I were driving in a car and at a turn in the road my father had signalled to us, and when we stopped he came running to catch us up. He was happy, he had a joyful smile as he climbed into the back of the car, for he had been let out of hospital that morning. I wrote to my mother that perhaps there was some truth in the idea of purgatory, and this was the moment of release.

For me this dream was the end of a series which had recurred over the years after his death. In them my father was always shut away in hospital out of touch with his wife and children – though sometimes he returned home on a visit, a silent solitary man, not really cured, who would have to go back again into exile. The dreams remain vivid even today, so that sometimes it is an effort for me to realize that there was no hospital, no separation, and that he lived with my mother till he died. In his last years he had diabetes and always beside her place at table there stood a weighing-machine to measure his diet, and it was she who daily gave him his injections of insulin. There was no truth at all in the idea of his loneliness and unhappiness, but perhaps the dreams show that I loved him more than I knew.

EARLY MORNING FEED

The father darts out on the stairs
To listen to that keening
In the upper room, for a change of note
That signifies distress, to scotch disaster,
The kettle humming in the room behind.

He thinks, on tiptoe, ears a-strain,
The cool dawn rising like the moon:
'Must not appear and pick him up;
He mustn't think he has me springing
To his beck and call,'
The kettle rattling behind the kitchen door.

He has him springing
A-quiver on the landing –
For a distress-note, a change of key,
To gallop up the stairs to him
To take him up, light as a violin,
And stroke his back until he smiles.
He sidles in the kitchen
And pours his tea . . .

And again stands hearkening
For milk cracking the lungs.
There's a little panting,
A cough: the thumb's in: he'll sleep,
The cup of tea cooling on the kitchen table.

Can he go in now to his chair and think
Of the miracle of breath, pick up a book,
Ready at all times to take it at a run
And intervene between him and disaster,
Sipping his cold tea as the sun comes up?

He returns to bed
And feels like something, with the door ajar,
Crouched in the bracken, alert, with big eyes
For the hunter, death, disaster.

Peter Redgrove (1932–   )

Trust yourself. You know more than you think you do. ... It may surprise you to hear that the more people have studied different methods of bringing up children the more they have come to the conclusion that what good mothers and fathers instinctively feel like doing for their babies is usually best.

Benjamin Spock, *Baby and Child Care*, 1955

Margaret Drabble shares with Charles Dickens credit for having changed social conditions as well as pleasing her readers. In 1965, when The Millstone *appeared, many English hospitals were still being run more like military institutions than places of healing. A London paediatrician told me that it did a great deal to change the attitudes of both hospital staff and parents, who became more ready*

*to trust their own instincts and make a fuss. In this extract
we see the (unmarried) mother of a baby taken into
hospital for an investigation arriving to visit the baby.*

The two nurses looked at each other, nervously, as
though I were a case.

'You're not allowed to visit in this ward,' one of
them said, with timid politeness, propitiating, kind, as
one speaks to the sick or the mad.

'I don't really care,' I said, 'whether I'm allowed to
visit or not. If you'll tell me where it is, I'll get there by
myself, and you needn't even say you saw me.'

'I'm afraid we can't possibly do that,' the other one
said when the first speaker said nothing. Like her
friend, she had a timid, undetermined note in her voice,
and I felt mean to pursue my point. I did pursue it,
however; I told them I had no intention of not seeing
my baby, that I didn't think it would upset her at all,
but that on the contrary it would cheer her up, and
cheer me up, and was in every way desirable, and that if
they didn't tell me how to find her I would just go and
look for myself. No, no, I couldn't possibly do that,
they both said at once, their voices hardening from
personal timidity and embarrassment into the weight of
authority. . . .

'I must see her,' I repeated. 'If you won't let me, go
and get Sister, or Matron, or whatever she's called. Go
and fetch her for me. Or I'll wait here till she comes.'

'She won't be here till two,' said one, and the other
said, 'You can't wait here, you aren't allowed to wait.'

'What do you mean, I'm not allowed?' I said crossly,
suffering greatly from this as yet mild degree of self-
assertion. 'Who doesn't allow me? Who says I can't
wait?'

'Sister won't see anyone anyway, at this time of day,'
they said. 'And she says that no one must be allowed to
wait.'

They began to look frightened; I could see that they were going to get into trouble if I were still there when Sister came back. I was sorry for them, but not as sorry as I was for Octavia [her baby]. I sat down on the desk and I waited. After five minutes one of them disappeared, perhaps in an effort to find someone more persuasive to dislodge me, but before she returned Sister arrived, and the remaining girl had to bear the brunt of her wrath.

'Well, well, Mrs Stacey,' she said snappily as she bustled in. 'So you're here again, are you? Now then, Miss Richards, how many times have I told you that this isn't a convenient time for visitors? Mrs Stacey, I'm afraid that I can't possibly talk . . .'

'I don't want to discuss anything,' I said. 'I've come to visit my baby.'

I felt happier now; I had not enjoyed upsetting those unimpressive nurses, whose discomfort in the situation had been almost as great as mine. In Sister, however, I sensed the kind of will that can be fought: she found pleasure, not torment, in assertion, so I felt free to assert myself too.

'I told you this morning,' said Sister, 'that visiting is quite out of the question.'

'I don't care what you told me,' I said. 'I want to see my baby. If you don't take me straight there, I shall walk round until I find the way myself. She's not kept under lock and key, I assume?'

'Miss Stacey,' said Sister, 'you are behaving most foolishly, and I must ask you to leave at once.'

'I won't leave,' I said. 'You'd much better take me straight there, I don't want to be compelled to wander round upsetting the whole of your hospital until I find my baby.'

'Now then, now then,' said Sister, 'this is neither the time nor the place for hysterical talk like that. We must all be grateful that your child is . . .'

'Grateful,' I said. 'I am grateful. I admire your hospital, I admire your work, I am devoted to the National Health Service. Now I want to see my baby.'

She came over to me and took my arm and started to push me gently towards the door . . . when she started to push, I started to scream . . .

*

Eventually they got me to sit down, but I went on screaming and moaning and keeping my eyes shut; through the noise I could hear things happening, people coming and going, someone slapped my face, someone tried to put a wet flannel on my head, and all the time I was thinking I must go on doing this until they let me see her. . . . After a while I heard someone shouting above the din, 'For God's sake tell her she can see the baby, someone try and tell her,' and I heard these words and instantly stopped and opened my eyes and beheld the stricken, confused silence around me.

'Did you say I could see the baby?' I said.

'Of course you can see the baby,' said Mr Protheroe. 'Of course you can see the baby. I cannot imagine why you should ever have been prevented from seeing the baby.'

I looked at the breathless circle surrounding me, which had changed its composition considerably since I had last seen it: Mr Protheroe himself looked agitated and white with anger, Sister was sitting in a corner and crying into a handkerchief, the nurses were looking stunned, and there were a couple more men also looking angry. It was as though I had opened my eyes on a whole narrative caught in a single picture, a narrative in which I myself had taken no part; it had been played out between the Sister and the others, quite clearly, and she had lost and was now suffering her defeat. It was nothing to do with me at all, I felt; I shut my eyes, wearily, upon them, for I did not want to know. I had no interest in their story; I wished to know only my own. I felt I could no longer bother to endure their conflicts; if I had gained my point, that was enough for me.'

'Can I go now and see my baby?' I asked.

'I will take you myself,' said Mr Protheroe, and I got up, and he took my arm and conducted me down the corridor.

In the course of a child-care study, four different mothers remark on their feelings for their children.

They've all of them bin a surprise – I never wanted none of them, and specially this last one. And I don't mind admitting, I've taken pills and pills, but I never got shut of none of 'em yet.

We didn't want none of 'em, come to that. They was all accidents. But we was *really* surprised to see Vicky, because we was using something before her.

They said I couldn't stand the weight of carrying. Well – I was *determined* to have a baby, so I said to Jack, 'We'll just go ahead and have one, and we won't tell anyone or ask anyone's advice.' So we did. I never saw any doctor or clinic or anyone right through until I called the midwife when he started. He was ten pounds and twenty-four inches long. Oh, it was fine, I wouldn't have missed it for the world. ... But we had to keep waking the midwife up with cups of tea, I was her fifth in forty-eight hours.

Nowadays, if they don't turn out right you wonder where *you've* gone wrong, don't you? It used to be, they made you do this and that, and you did it, and if things went wrong it was the child's fault, not the parents', they could never be wrong. I think we're not so happy about *ourselves* these days, we blame ourselves, not the child. I do, I know. I wish I didn't sometimes.

From John and Elizabeth Newson, *Infant Care in an Urban Community*, 1963

§

THIS BE THE VERSE

> They fuck you up, your mum and dad,
>> They may not mean to, but they do.
> They fill you with the faults they had
>> And add some extra, just for you.
>
> But they were fucked up in their turn
>> By fools in old-style hats and coats,
> Who half the time were soppy-stern
>> And half at one another's throats.
>
> Man hands on misery to man.
>> It deepens like a coastal shelf.
> Get out as early as you can,
>> And don't have any kids yourself.

Philip Larkin (1922–)

Here is a flawlessly honest account of the price we pay for living close to our children, divesting ourselves of remoteness and moral authority. It is the other side of the coin represented by the Samuel Butler extract: victim and tormentor have exchanged roles.

Standing by the toaster, Erica contemplates her children, whom she once thought the most beautiful beings on earth. Jeffrey's streaked blond hair hangs tangled and unwashed over his eyes in front and his collar in back; he hunches awkwardly above the table, cramming fried egg into his mouth and chewing noisily. Matilda, who is wearing a peevish expression and an orange tie-dyed jersey which looks as if it had been spat on, is stripping the crusts off her toast with her fingers. Chomp, crunch, scratch.

How has it all come about? She is – or at least she was – a gentle, rational, even-tempered woman, not given to violent feelings. In her whole life she cannot remember disliking anyone as much as she now sometimes dislikes Jeffrey and Matilda.

They were a happy family once, she thinks. Jeffrey and Matilda were beautiful, healthy babies; charming toddlers; intelligent, lively, affectionate children. There are photograph albums and folders of drawings and stories and report cards to prove it. Then last year, when Jeffrey turned fourteen and Matilda twelve, they had begun to change; to grow rude, course, selfish, insolent, nasty, brutish, and tall. It was as if she were keeping a boarding house in a bad dream, and the children she had loved were turning into awful lodgers – lodgers who paid no rent, whose leases could not be terminated. They were awful at home and abroad; in company and alone; in the morning, the afternoon, and the evening.

Though equally awful, the children are awful in somewhat different ways. Jeffrey is sullen, restless, and intermittently violent. Matilda is sulky, lazy, and intermittently dishonest. Jeffrey is obsessed with inventions and space; Matilda with clothes and pop music. Matilda is extravagant and wasteful; Jeffrey miserly and ungenerous. Jeffrey is still doing all right in school, while his sister's grades are hopeless; on the other hand, Matilda is generally much cleaner than Jeffrey.

Erica knows and remembers that Jeffrey and Matilda had once loved her. They had loved Brian. Now they quite evidently do not like either of their parents. They also do not like each other: they fight constantly, and pick on each other for their respective failings.

The worst part of it all is that the children are her fault. All the authorities and writers say so. In their innocent past Erica and Brian had blamed their own short-comings on their parents while retaining credit for their own achievements. They had passed judgment on the character of acquaintances whose young children were not as nice as Muffy and Jeffo – But everyone did that. To have had disagreeable parents excused one's faults; to have disagreeable children underlined them. The parents might not look especially guilty; they might seem outwardly to be intelligent, kind, and charming people – but underneath were Mr and Mrs Hyde.

The fact that they had been quite all right until last year was no excuse. Erica had read widely on the subject, and knew that there were several bad explanations of this. Only last week she came across an article which spoke of the tendency of women who marry older men to remain, and wish to remain, children. (Brian is now forty-six, seven years older than she.) It was pointed out that such women tended to identify closely, 'even symbiotically' with their children. The author of this article would probably say that Jeffrey and Matilda are now struggling to break out of a symbiotic neurosis. Other experts might maintain that Erica has bewitched them out of spite and envy of their youth, energy, and 'emerging sexuality'; while still others would assert that the children have been assigned to work out her and Brian's repressed anti-social drives. And any or all of these experts might be right. Erica is not aware of these motives in herself, but that does not prove anything; naturally, they would not be conscious.

It is all academic by now, because now she consciously dislikes her children, and this alone would be

enough to poison them spiritually, morally, and emotionally. She dislikes them for being what they now are,
and for having turned her into a hateful, neurotic,
guilty person.

Alison Lurie, *The War Between the Tates*, 1974

*Binny, like Erica in the previous extract, is defenceless
before her children. On this occasion she is trying to get
them to go out while she gives a dinner party intended to
impress her somewhat conventional lover and his friends.
She is urging Lucy, the elder, to take Alison, the younger,
to the neighbours who have offered to have her for the
night.*

'Alison won't,' said Lucy, coming back into the room.

'Well, make her,' shouted Binny, stamping her foot.
She was beginning to breathe quite heavily. 'I would be
grateful if you would get your own things together as
well. Have you got your nightdress?'

'Don't be bloody wet,' said Lucy. She went to the
table and tore at a french loaf with her teeth.

'I don't want to remind you of the shirt I bought you,'
Binny said. 'Or the pair of shoes costing twenty-four
pounds that you said you couldn't live without and
promptly gave to your friend Soggy. When I was your
age I was grateful if my mother gave me a smile.'

'I lent them, you fool,' corrected Lucy.

Binny's voice became shrill. 'I've long since given up
expecting gratitude or common courtesy, but I do
expect you to get Alison and yourself out of the house.
It's little enough to ask, God knows.'

'Keep your lid on,' said Lucy. She began to comb
her hair at the mirror. Strands of hair and crumbs of
bread fell to the hearth. Binny could feel a pulse beating
in her throat. She burned with fury. No wonder she
never put on an ounce of weight. The daily aggravation
the children caused her was probably comparable to a

five-mile run or an hour with the skipping rope. Clutching the region of her heart and fighting for self-control, she said insincerely, 'Darling, you can be very sensitive and persuasive. Just tell her Sybil's waiting and that there's ice cream and things.'

Lucy strolled into the hall and called loudly, 'Come down, Alison, or I'll bash your teeth in.'

After several minutes a sound of barking was heard on the first-floor landing.

'Baby,' crooned Binny, going upstairs with out-stretched arms. Alison was on all fours, crouched against the wall. Binny often told friends it was nothing to worry about. Until two years ago Alison had insisted on baring her tummy button in the street and rubbing it against lamp posts. She had grown out of that, as doubtless she would soon grow tired of pretending she was a dog.

'Come along, darling,' said Binny brightly. She bent down and patted her daughter's head.

Alison growled and seized Binny's ankle in her teeth.

Putting both hands behind her to resist hitting the child, Binny descended the stairs.

Lucy was at the sink pouring cooking sherry into a milk bottle.

'Out, out, out,' cried Binny. 'I am not here to provide booze for your layabout friends. This is not an off-licence.'

She frogmarched Lucy to the door and pushed her down the steps. Alison began to cry. Running down the path, Binny caught up with Lucy at the hedge and put desperate arms about her. She said urgently, 'Now please, pull yourself together. Get your things, take your coat, and I'll give you a pound note to spend.'

Smirking, Lucy re-entered the house and began to put on her flying jacket. Smothering her youngest daughter in kisses, Binny took her to the door. She nodded blindly as Alison climbed the fence.

'You're crying, Mummy,' called Alison. Her mouth quivered.

'I'm very happy, darling,' said Binny. 'Don't you worry about me.' She wiped her cheeks with her hand. 'I'm going to have a lovely party.' She stood there waving until Alison was let into the Evans's.

Lucy had locked herself in the bathroom. Binny blew crumbs off the tablecloth and attended to the cushions on the sofa. She cut the end off the mutilated loaf and straightened the reproduction of The Last Supper that hung askew on the wall. Then she called gently down the hall that she would like to use the lavatory.

'Go away,' snarled Lucy. 'I'm trying to have a crap.'

Binny left a pound note on the table and climbed the stairs. She walked round and round her bedroom humming fiercely. . . .

After a time Lucy shouted that she was off now. Binny kept silent:

'Well, come on. Give us a kiss.'

'I certainly won't,' called Binny. 'You're far too rude.'

The door slammed violently. Instantly remorseful, Binny ran to the window and watched her daughter walk sullenly along the gutter. She looked such a little girl, aggressively scuffing the ground with the studs of her massive boots. At the same age Binny had been married and looking after a house. She rapped frantically on the pane of glass; she blew kisses. Lucy disappeared round the corner.

Beryl Bainbridge, *Injury Time*, 1977

WHEN I WAS YOUR AGE

When I was your age, child –
When I was eight,
When I was ten,
When I was two
(How old are you?) –
When I was your age, child,
My father would have gone quite *wild*
Had I behaved the way you
Do.
What, food uneaten on my plate
When I was eight?
What, room in such a filthy state
When I was ten?
What, late
For school when I was two?
My father would have shouted, 'When
I was your age, child, my father would have *raved*
Had I behaved
The way you
Do.'

When I was
Your age, child, I did not drive us
All perpetually mad
By bashing
Up my little brother and reducing him to tears.
There was a war on in those years!
There were no brothers to be had!
Even sisters were on ration!
My goodness, we were pleased
To get *anything* to tease!
We were glad
Of aunts and dogs,
Of chickens, grandmothers, and frogs;
Of creatures finned and creatures hooved,
And second cousins twice removed!

When I was your
Age, child, I was more
Considerate of others
(Particularly of fathers and of mothers).
I did not sprawl
Reading the Dandy
Or the Beano
When aunts and uncles came to call.
Indeed no.
I grandly
Entertained them all
With 'Please,' and 'Thank you,' 'May I . . .?'
        'Thank you,' 'Sorry,' 'Please,'
And other remarks like these.
And if a chance came in the conversation
I would gracefully recite a line
Which everyone recognised as a quotation
From one of the higher multiplication
Tables, like 'Seven sevens are forty-nine.'

When I was your age, child, I
Should never have dreamed
Of sitting idly
Watching television half the night.
It would have seemed
Demented:
Television not then having been
Invented.
When I
Was your age, child, I did not lie
About
The house all day.
(I did not lie about anything at all – no liar I!)
I got out!
I ran away!
To sea!
(Though naturally I was back, with hair brushed and
        hands washed, in time for tea.)
Oh yes, goodness me,
When I was nine
I had worked already down a diamond mine,
And fought in several minor wars,
And hunted boars
In the lonelier
Parts of Patagonia.
(Though I admit that possibly by then
I was getting on for ten.)
In the goldfields of Australia
I learned the bitterness of failure;
Experience in the temples of Siam
Made me the wise and punctual man I am;
But the lesson that I value most
I learned upon the Coromandel Coast –
Never, come what may, to boast.

When
I was your age, child, and the older generation
Offered now and then
A kindly explanation
Of what the world was like in their young day
I did not yawn in that rude way.
Why, goodness me,
There being no television to see
(As I have, I think, already said)
We were dashed grateful
For any entertainment we could get instead,
However tedious and hateful.

So grow up, child! And be
Your age! (What *is* your age, then?
Eight? Or nine? Or two? Or ten?)
Remember, as you look at me –
When I was your age I was forty-three.

Michael Frayn, taken from *Allsorts* (a children's annual)

Acknowledgements

The editor and publishers gratefully acknowledge permission to use copyright material in this book:

John Aubrey: Extract from *Brief Lives*, edited by Oliver Lawson Dick. Reprinted by permission of Martin Secker & Warburg Ltd.

Beryl Bainbridge: Extract from *Injury Time*. Reprinted by permission of Gerald Duckworth & Co. Ltd.

Margaret Drabble: Extract from *The Millstone*. Reprinted by permission of George Weidenfeld & Nicolson Ltd.

Michael Frayn: From *Allsorts*, edited by Ann Thwaite. Reprinted by permission of Elaine Greene Ltd., for the author.

Graham Greene: Extract from *A Sort of Life* (The Bodley Head/ Simon & Schuster). Copyright © 1971 by Graham Greene. Reprinted by permission of Laurence Pollinger Ltd., and Simon & Schuster, a Division of Gulf & Western Corp.

Philip Larkin: From *High Windows*, copyright © 1974 by Philip Larkin. Reprinted by permission of Faber & Faber Ltd., and Farrar, Straus & Giroux, Inc.

Alison Lurie: Extract from *The War Between the Tates*. Copyright © 1974 by Alison Lurie. Reprinted by permission of Wm. Heinemann Ltd., and Random House, Inc.

Naomi Mitchison: Extract from *Small Talk* (The Bodley Head). Reprinted by permission of David Higham Associates Ltd.

J. & E. Newson: Extract from *Infant Care in an Urban Community*. Reprinted by permission of George Allen & Unwin.

William Plomer: Extract from *Double Lives*. Reprinted by permission of Jonathan Cape Ltd., for the Estate of William Plomer.

Peter Redgrove: From *The Collector and Other Poems* (1959). Reprinted by permission of Routledge & Kegan Paul Ltd.

Benjamin Spock: Extract from *Baby and Child Care*. Reprinted by permission of The Bodley Head & Laurence Pollinger Ltd., and Pocket Books, New York.

Virginia Woolf: Extract from *To the Lighthouse*. Copyright 1927 by Harcourt Brace Jovanovich, Inc., copyright 1955 by Leonard Woolf. Reprinted by permission of The Hogarth Press for the Author's Literary Estate, and Harcourt Brace Jovanovich, Inc.

ACKNOWLEDGEMENTS

W. B. Yeats: Extract from 'A Prayer for my Daughter' from *Collected Poems*. Copyright 1924 by Macmillan Publ. Co. Inc., renewed 1952 by Bertha Georgie Yeats. Reprinted by permission of A. P. Watt Ltd., for M. B. Yeats, Anne Yeats and Macmillan, London, and by permission of Macmillan Publ. Co., Inc.

While every effort has been made to secure permission, we may have failed in a few cases to trace the copyright holder. We apologize for any apparent negligence.

The illustrations in this book were taken from E. N. Marks, *Pictures and Readings for Little Learners* (London, 1872). Courtesy of Brian Rees-Williams.

Index of Authors

84-3214 McL

DATE		
FEB 2 8 1994		

84-3214 McL

LOR CO.